WORLD CULTURES IN PERSPECTIVE

THE ANCIENT NEAR EAST

Harry A. Dawe

CHARLES E. MERRILL PUBLISHING CO.
A Bell & Howell Company
Columbus, Ohio

Author

Harry A. Dawe is currently serving as Headmaster at The Harvey School in Katonah, New York. His previous professional experience includes the Assistant Headmastership at The Beaver Country Day School in Chestnut Hill, Massachusetts, where he also taught and served as Chairman of the History Department. Mr. Dawe received his B.A. degree from Oberlin College and his M.A. degree from Columbia University. He is the author of *Ancient Greece and Rome* in Merrill's World Cultures in Perspective series. He has contributed a number of articles to professional journals and is a member of the American Historical Association and the New England History Teachers' Association.

Acknowledgements

Thanks are due the following authors and publishers for permission to reprint the material on the pages indicated: p. 7: Carleton Coon, *The Story of Man* (Alfred A. Knopf, Inc., 1954); reprinted by permission of the publisher. p. 7: A. L. Kroeber and Clyde Kluckhohn, eds., "Culture: A Critical Review of Concepts and Definitions," *Papers of the Peabody Museum of American Archaeology and Ethnology* (Harvard University, XLVII, No. 1, 1952); reprinted by permission of the publisher. p. 8: William Howells, *Back of History* (New York: Doubleday & Co., Inc., Anchor Books, 1963); reprinted by permission of the author. p. 23: H. S. Commager, ed., *Documents of American History* (New York: Appleton-Century-Crofts, Inc., 1953). p. 30: Herbert J. Muller, *Freedom in the Ancient World* (New York: Harper & Row, Publishers, Inc., Bantam Books, 1964); reprinted by permission of the publisher. pp. 32-33, 41, 53: Reprinted from *The Intellectual Adventure of Ancient Man* by H. A. Frankfort, et al., by permission of The University of Chicago Press. Copyright 1946 by The University of Chicago. All rights reserved. Published 1946. Composed and printed by The University of Chicago Press, Chicago, Illinois, U.S.A. pp. 39, 43, 44, 47-48, 48: Samuel N. Kramer, *History Begins at Sumer* (Indian Hills, Colorado: The Falcon's Wing Press, 1956); reprinted by permission of the author. pp. 41-42, 62, 120-121, 138: Sabatino Moscati, *The Face of the Ancient Orient* (New York: Doubleday & Co., Inc., 1962); reprinted by permission of Quadrangle Books, Inc. p. 43: Samuel N. Kramer, *Sumerian Mythology* (Philadelphia: The American Philosophical Society, 1944); reprinted by permission. pp. 45-46, 64-65, 67, 69-73, 78, 85, 93, 93-94, 95, 96-97, 99-101, 103-106, 107-111: James B. Pritchard, ed., *Ancient Near Eastern Texts Relating to the Old Testament*. Reprinted by permission of Princeton University Press, copyright, 1950, 1955, by Princeton University Press, second edition, 1955. pp. 49-50: Leonard Cottrell, *The Anvil of Civilization* (New York: The New American Library, Inc., Mentor Books, 1957); reprinted by permission of the publisher. p. 56: J. Hawkes and L. Wolley, *History of Mankind: Pre-History and the Beginnings of Civilization* (New York: Harper & Row, Publishers, Inc., 1963); reprinted by permission of the publisher. p. 61: Henri Frankfort, *Ancient Egyptian Religion* (New York: Columbia University Press, 1948); reprinted by permission of the publisher. p. 63: T. Eric Peet, trans., *A Comparative Study of the Literature of Egypt, Palestine and Mesopotamia* (London: Oxford University Press, 1931). pp. 66-67: Miriam Lichtheim, trans., "The Songs of the Harpers," *Journal of Near Eastern Studies*, IV, No. 3 (1945); reprinted by permission of The University of Chicago Press. pp. 80-81, 81-84: N. K. Sandars, *The Epic of Gilgamesh* (Harmondsworth, Middlesex, England: Penguin Books, Ltd., 1960); reprinted by permission of the publisher. All biblical quotations: *The Holy Bible*, Revised Standard Version (New York: Thomas Nelson & Sons, 1953).

ISBN 0-675-01280-5

Copyright © 1969 by
CHARLES E. MERRILL PUBLISHING CO.
A Bell & Howell Company
Columbus, Ohio 43216

All rights reserved. No part of this book may be reproduced in any form, by any method whatsoever, without permission in writing from the publisher.
Printed in the United States of America

Preface

The study of history can be thorough and detached but never totally inclusive or objective. Therefore, this book is a selective and interpretive narrative rather than a chronicle of events. It has been conceived in the belief that an interpretive account is a kind of cutting edge which provokes critical thinking and provides a flexible instrument of instruction. The book is not dogmatic but rather offers the intellectual tools which can be used in the development of individual analysis and judgment. Raw material for interpretation has been provided in the various illustrations and in the form of primary documents placed both in the body of the text and in the collection of Readings at the ends of the units. The Readings form an integral part of the text and are designed to be read in conjunction with the appropriate chapters.

The spatial and temporal limits of the book are the Near East from man's origins to approximately 500 B.C. Some Near Eastern phenomena such as Islam and Christianity are excluded from the book, but they will be covered elsewhere in the series. Hopefully, the only bias in this account is the belief that the fundamental human condition remains constant. Ancillary to this belief is the assumption that the progress made by successive generations removes problems but at the same time produces new ones. Therefore, there is a basic equality of human civilization regardless of time and place. This book attempts to throw some light on one manifestation of the phenomenon of man.

Throughout the preparation of this book, students, colleagues and friends have given valuable criticism and advice. Specific thanks are here publicly expressed to the Headmaster and Trustees of The Beaver Country Day School, and especially to Sumner Gerstein, for their support of the project, to my colleague, Werner Heider, for the benefit of his erudition and to my friend, John Martin, for his informed criticism. Thanks are also expressed to Dale Kittle, who is both proofreader and typist, and to Jean Diederich Stouffer of Charles E. Merrill Publishing, who provided admirable support and advice throughout the process of publication. Greatest thanks go to my wife, Patt, who bore with grace the vicissitudes of writing.

Harry A. Dawe
Boston, Massachusetts

Table of Contents

UNIT I Before Civilization

Chapter 1	Evolution and the Culture of Man	2
Chapter 2	Paleolithic and Neolithic Culture	13
Chapter 3	Civilization	26
Reading I	Mythological Thought	32

UNIT II The Creation of Civilization

Chapter 4	Sumer	36
Chapter 5	Egypt	52
Reading II	"The Story of Sinuhe"	69

UNIT III The Elaboration of Civilization

Chapter 6	Babylonia and Beyond	76
Chapter 7	Imperial Egypt	91
Reading III	The Code of Hammurabi	103
Reading IV	The Babylonian Creation Story	107

UNIT IV The Spread of Civilization

Chapter 8	The Small Nations	114
Chapter 9	The Great Empires	126

UNIT V The Revolution Within Civilization: Israel

Chapter 10	The Development of Monotheism	144
Chapter 11	The Universal God of History	158
Reading V	Selections from the Old Testament	167

Epilogue: The Legacy of the Near East	179
Index	190

Maps

The Creation of Civilization (c. 3000 B.C.)	20
The Near East (c. 2000-1500 B.C.)	66
The Near East (c. 1000-600 B.C.)	118
The Persian Empire (c. 500 B.C.)	136
The Extent of Civilization (c. 500 B.C.)	164

Before we can begin to study the history of man and the development of civilization, we must first find out something about man himself. We must see him at his origin, discover and trace his main characteristics and look at his life on earth before he created civilization. A trip to the zoo and a brief look at apes or monkeys will quickly show that man is similar to them. Apes and monkeys have traits which seem almost human: semi-erect posture, forelimbs which serve as hands, good eyesight, and the ability to make distinct vocal sounds. Yet the human animal must have some different characteristics and abilities, or <u>he</u> would be in the zoo. How, then, is man different from the rest of the animal kingdom? In other words, what kind of animal is man?

UNIT 1
Before Civilization

1

Evolution and the Culture of Man

The people most interested in finding out what kind of animal man is are called *anthropologists;* the word *anthropology* itself means knowledge of man. To learn about man, anthropologists study living men and animals and the fossil remains of men and animals who lived millions of years ago. They also study the things which man has made and the ideas and customs which he has developed and perhaps written down. Through such studies, they know that during the long history of the earth, animal life has changed a great deal as conditions on the earth have changed. Most anthropologists believe that the various forms of life now existing on the earth, including man, did not always exist. Also, many species of animals which once existed in the distant past are no longer around. This constant changing of nature took place over millions of years and is still going on, so slowly that we hardly notice it. Any gradual change such as this is called *evolution*.

Evolution

It is generally believed that the earth was originally a mass of very hot matter. Over a period of billions of years, it gradually cooled. During this long cooling period, the climate of the earth changed. The Sahara Desert, for example, was at one time a moist area covered with rich vegetation. During these climate changes, animal life evolved into different forms to adapt to new conditions. Those animals who failed to change rapidly or thoroughly enough became extinct. The dinosaurs, for example, had certain characteristics which made it difficult for them to survive when the amount of vegetation on the earth declined. Other animals—the horseshoe crab is one—have survived for millions of years without changing their appearance. Still others have endured but have become changed versions of their ancestors. Man is thought to be one such animal.

Primates. The class of animals which anthropologists call the *primates* are those who are the most intelligent and most versatile of the animals, those most capable of adapting to different conditions. Apes, monkeys and human beings are primates. Long before man appeared on earth, according to the theory, ape-like animals were living in trees, utilizing those traits most suited for tree living. Two such traits were three-dimensional vision and free-moving forearms. As the earth changed and grasslands appeared, some primates moved down from the trees. Those who survived on the ground were those capable of best using the traits necessary for survival in the grasslands. Such traits were erect posture, long-range vision and quick intelligence. According to some anthropologists, the primates who over the centuries developed and used these traits became the ancestors of man.

Just when this descent from the trees took place is, of course, difficult to determine; twenty million years ago would be a rough estimate. Only about one million years ago, it is thought, certain primates appeared who had man-like characteristics. Fossils of these primates have been found. These creatures stood erect and had fingers and thumbs and large brains. Anthropologists call these creatures *hominids* and have named each variety after the places where their bones have been found. Examples include the Peking man, Rhodesian man, Java man, Neanderthal man and Cro-Magnon man.

The Appearance of *Homo Sapiens*. Scientists believe that the gradual extinction of all hominids but one type occurred during what is called the Ice Age, which began about 700,000 years ago. During a period of hundreds of thousands of years, the temperature of the earth changed, causing four ice ages. During these ice ages, most of the earth was covered with a huge glacier. As a result of the periodic advance and retreat of the ice sheet, the climate and topography of the earth changed a great deal. In response to changing conditions, species of animal life either underwent a change or died out. Anthropologists believe that by the end of the last ice age, or about 35,000 years ago, only one species of hominid remained. He is the hominid which anthropologists

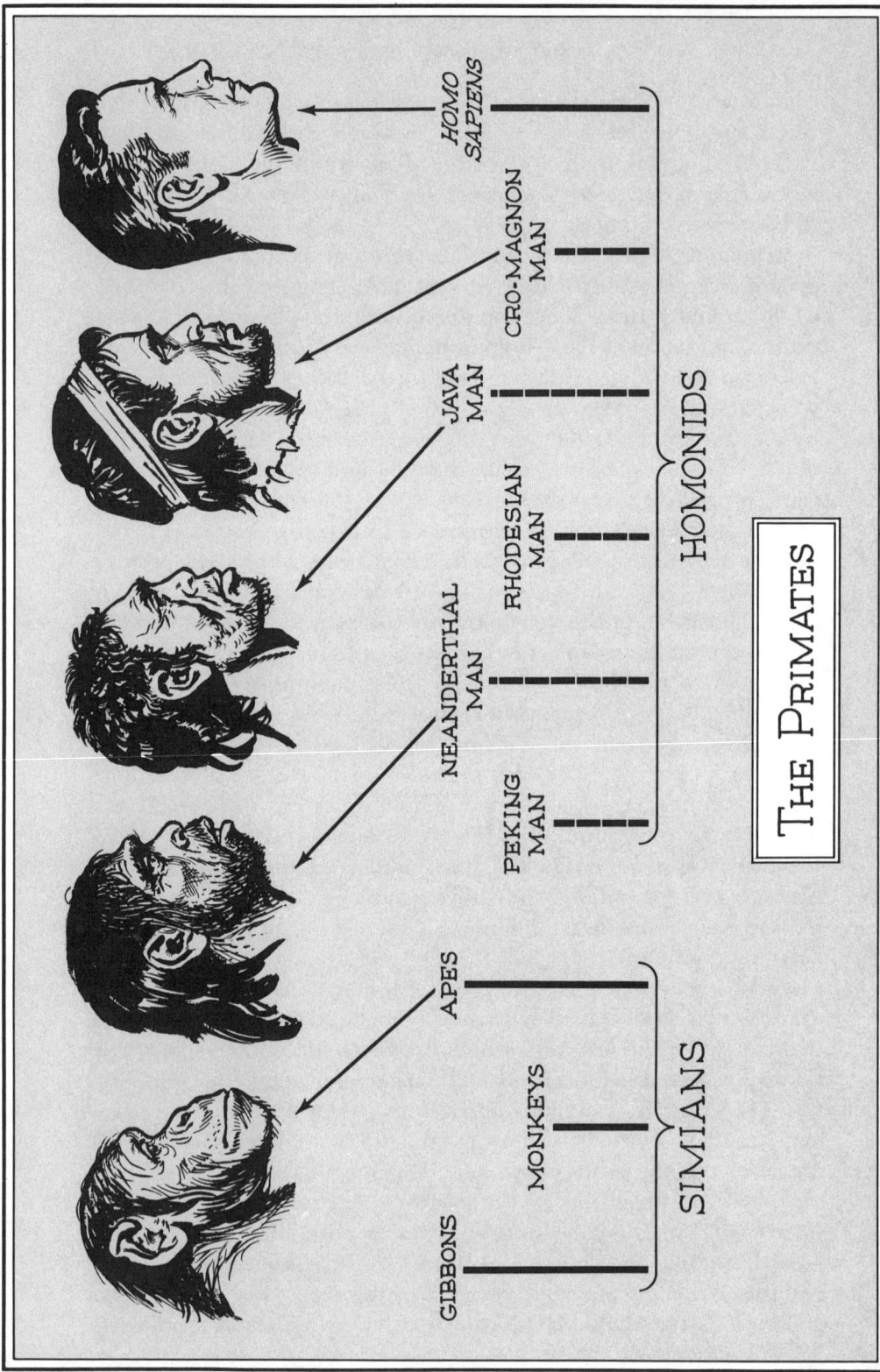

often call *homo sapiens,* or "man the thinker." Modern man is *homo sapiens.*

This brief sketch of man's physical evolution is based upon work done by people called *physical anthropologists.* As their name suggests, these people study the physical structure of modern man, modern primates and the few bones of early hominids which have been dug up from the distant past. However, the evolution of man is not as simple or certain a thing as this brief explanation would indicate. Anthropologists do not really know how or why one kind of primate changed its physical structure to what we see today in the human body. They are not sure whether modern man is a changed version of an earlier hominid or a totally different species related to a much earlier primate. Recent theory teaches, however, that man is not descended from the apes but rather is related to them, having a common ancestor.

The evidence is so scanty that there are many missing links in the evolutionary chain. Nevertheless, to many anthropologists, the theory seems probable and, in fact, almost certain. New discoveries are being made all the time. With each uncovering of a bone or jaw from prehistoric times, something more is learned about the evolution of man and therefore more is known about his nature. Through this kind of study, we learn more about ourselves.

The Development of Culture

If man were merely a creature capable of physical evolution, he would today be no better than an intelligent ape, although at times, he has seemed to be no more than that. Scientists, observing modern primates (especially gibbons and chimpanzees), have been impressed by their intelligence, their ability to communicate and their ability to form a kind of social organization. These primates seem to have a set of rules for living together, and to this extent, they are like humans. Yet man has something else; it is this "something else" which distinguishes him from other primates. A standard religious explanation is to call this "something else" a soul. Another approach is to say that man has a unique kind of intelligence which takes the place of instinct in animals. Whatever the cause of man's superiority, it explains the existence of art, language, machinery, religion and thousands of other activities which are unknown to even the most advanced nonhuman primates. The word chosen by most people to describe these distinctive human activities is *culture*. Those who study this aspect of man, the things he has created rather than just his physical nature, are called *cultural anthropologists*.

A precise definition of culture is difficult to formulate. Instead of defining the term now, it might be wise for us to look at some things which only man can do, and then attempt to construct a definition. As the human animal evolved, he became physically weaker than many of the other animals. A human child, for instance, is dependent upon others for a considerable period of time after birth, whereas most animals are capable of independent survival at an early age. During this prolonged infancy, a human is capable of being taught things and so learns to put his brain to use.

The Transmission of Knowledge. Knowledge and the skills learned by one generation can be passed on to the next; in this process, the development of language is of the greatest importance. Words are agreed-upon sounds which can be used to stand for things, actions or ideas. Once learned, they can be remembered and applied to any situation. This ability enables the human to see situations before they occur and to anticipate solutions. These solutions can be passed on to other humans through the medium of language, and as a result of this activity, man can create a storehouse of knowledge which is constantly being increased.

When faced with a drop in temperature, an animal will react on the basis of instinct; it will either seek out a warm spot like a deep cave, or it will migrate to a warmer climate area. A man, on the other hand, can sense the cold, see a heavy coat of hair on an animal, kill the animal and use its hide to make a coat. Man can grasp the concept of coldness and the concept of coatmaking and connect the two.

Adaptability. Man can devise his own ways of organizing his society and can change them when necessary. This adaptability is a striking characteristic of man and can be seen in many of his activities. Apes have been known to pick up pieces of wood and use them to dig with, but it is only man who knows how to make tools in order to meet a specific need. Man is able to see the principle of leverage and to apply it in many ways, whereas an ape may stumble on to a stick, use it as a lever to move a stone, but be unable to apply the same principle in other ways or even to pass this skill on to other apes. Man can abstract an idea from observations, form a concept and then put this concept to use. From this basic ability has sprung all of man's inventions and his entire way of life.

The things which only man can do, and decides to do, make up his culture. Since man's intelligence permits individuals to make different decisions, his culture has infinite variety. Separate groups of the same kind of monkeys act the same everywhere, but separate groups of men act differently because each group has developed a distinct culture and continues to modify it. Because of this ability, man's culture has evolved and continues to evolve at a rapid pace, even though his physical form changes very slowly. Man is not tied to the slow natural processes of the lower animals; therefore, his history is one of *cultural evolution* rather than *physical evolution*.

Definition of Culture. With these ideas in mind, we can now look at one anthropologist's definition of culture.

> We may consider culture in general to be the sum total of the way in which human beings live, transmitted from generation to generation by learning. It includes the regulations between people in pairs and in groups, man's work activities involving natural materials and the expenditure of energy in the realm of symbols, including speech, music, the visual arts and the human body itself. *Culture is the sum total of the things that people do as a result of having been so taught.*

In spite of all the things which man has invented, there are some things which he has in common with the animals. According to one theory, these things may come from his pre-cultural, or animal, period. Man's reproductive instincts and his basic drive for food and water, as well as some of his aggressive tendencies, are common to humans and to animals. It has been said that the desire among children to climb trees to build houses in them is an indication of an instinct carried over from our tree-living ancestors. Yet the things which affect man most, things which shape his desires, fears, hopes and values, are part of the culture which previous thousands of generations of men have created and which man acquires when he is born and grows up.

A visit to the Far East would make perfectly clear to us the fact that in spite of common human characteristics, people in the United States live differently from people in the Far East.

> The way in which people in any group do things, make and use tools, get along with one another and with other groups, the words they use and the way they use them to express thoughts, and the thoughts they think—all of these we call the group's culture.

Culture is not only a collection of discoveries and inventions which have given man great power; it is also a system of values and beliefs which might well restrict our actions and prejudice our opinions. The reason we think and act the way we do can be found in the history of our own particular culture.

If we wish to cope with ourselves, we must learn to cope with our culture. As one writer has explained:

> ... people have never been very much aware that there was such a thing as culture. It goes back before history; it has seemingly always been there; they take it for granted. It actually grew up out of the sum of inventions and adjustments they happened to make, and it could not have followed exactly the same course for two different societies. So no two societies have the same culture. And each one thinks its own is the obvious and natural way of doing things. This is not simple preference; it is because human societies, unlike animal societies, are based upon their own cultures and cannot continue to exist as human societies without those particular cultures that have continually sustained them.

The Elements of Culture

Before we can see how man built his culture, we must stop for a moment and learn how we should go about studying human culture. The word culture encompasses everything which man has made, from shovels to poetry, and is too broad and abstract a term to use with any kind of precision. Therefore, it is necessary to break this word down into a few concrete parts—into four elements of culture.

Control of Environment. Man's *control of his environment* is the basic element of culture; it includes the way man feeds, houses and clothes himself and, in general, how he provides for his physical needs. In order to talk intelligibly about this element of culture, it is necessary to master two words: *economy* and *technology*. *Economy* is a word based upon a Greek word meaning household management; it describes the art of obtaining and distributing the wealth and resources which man takes from the physical world. *Technology* comes from two Greek words, *techne*, meaning craft, and *logia*, meaning knowledge of. Technology describes the actual methods used by man to obtain his physical resources. For example, the economic basis of Egyptian culture was agriculture; thus, an understanding of the Egyptian economy and its impact on the peoples' way of life is necessary to understand the Egyptian culture. The kinds of tools used to practice an agrarian economy, tools such as plows and hoes, as well as irrigation ditches, comprise Egyptian technology. To cite a modern example, the United States has an industrial economy, whereas India has an agricultural economy. Each nation has, then, a different way of controlling its environment.

Communication. A second element of culture is called *communication*. In this element, language is the most important activity, for without it, there would be no culture at all. One study of this part of culture, the study of words, is called *linguistics;* from it, much can be learned about human culture, our own Western culture included. Some people have no word for "war"; others have no word for "peace," and some have no word corresponding to our word for "love." Linguistic facts can tell much about a culture. In fact, one man, writing a book about three nations, described their entire culture from an analysis of their language!

In the Greek language, the word for river, *potamos*, is also related to the word for drink, a fact which should tell us something about the size and nature of Greek rivers. In our own culture, it is

For hunting and fighting, early civilized man relied on such weapons as these bronze and copper spearheads, dating from about 3000 B.C.

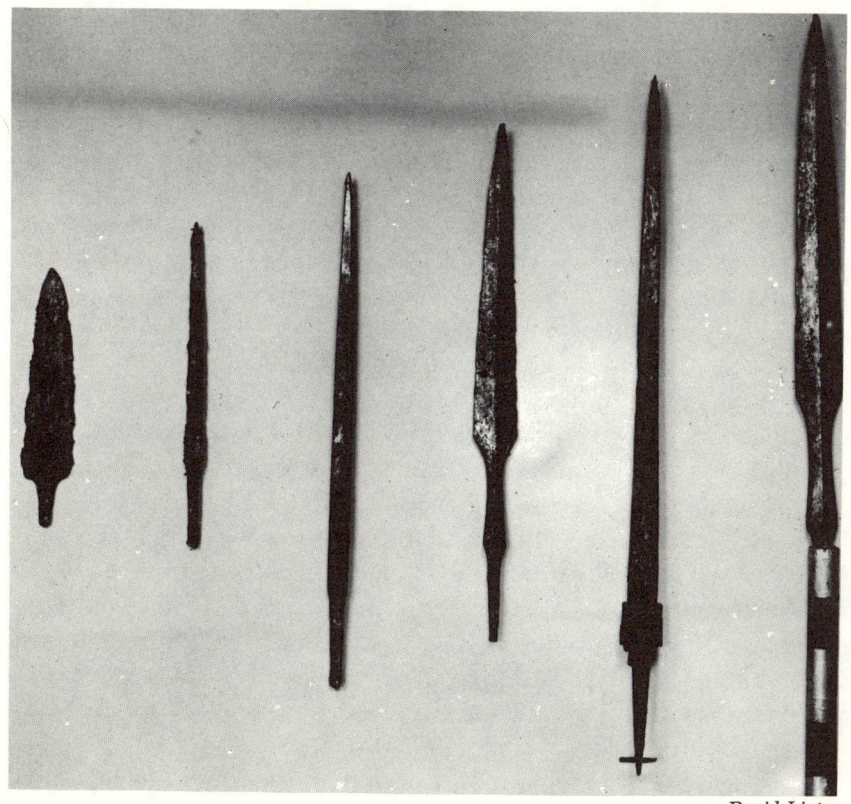

David Linton

significant that the slang word "cool" (rather than "hot") has been used to describe something good or desirable. Also, when we were about to put a man in space, it became apparent that our culture had no word to describe the "spaceman." We had to invent a word by combining two Greek words, and in so doing added to our culture. Studying the origin of this new word should, in itself, tell us something about the background of our own culture.

Cooperation. As we have seen, even animals are social creatures, for they gather in groups to work together. The third element of culture, *cooperation,* can be seen in human society in which rules and customs have been developed to permit individuals to live in some degree of harmony with each other. *Society* is the word used to describe the way in which people live with each other on a day-to-day basis—the way, for example, they raise and educate children and the way they decide what kinds of people will have important positions in relationship to others. In some cultures, religious leaders have the most important place in society, whereas in others, businessmen have more influential or respected positions. Such facts describe the *social structure* of a culture.

Politics is the term used to describe the way leaders are chosen and the manner in which individual desires and ambitions are regulated to meet the needs of the group. The political side of cooperation deals with the way a culture chooses to govern itself. For example, one group of people might choose leaders on the basis of military skill, another on the basis of intelligence and yet another on the basis of popularity. The political side of culture involves such questions as Who will make decisions? What group of people is able to coerce others?

The Use of Mind and Spirit. The fourth element of culture has to do with man's mind and spirit—that part of human activity which cannot be seen or touched. We call this last element *the use of mind and spirit.* Since, according to theory, the mind of the human primate was the driving force behind his cultural development in the first place, this element of culture is perhaps the most important of all. Once man developed his own culture, he separated himself somewhat from the natural process. He could now make his own environment, shape his own destiny and almost change the nature of his species by the power of his mind. He could use his mind to abstract ideas and to grasp the principles of things. Nature yielded to his intelligence.

As a result of this separation from nature, man had to face new problems. He had to decide what sort of creature he was, how and why he had been created and what his purpose in life was. Now that he could anticipate things which were not right in front of him, he had to cope with the anxiety which comes with sickness and with the knowledge that he would one day die. In other words, man was confronted with problems other than material ones such as food and shelter. He faced spiritual problems; he could now move in the world of his own imagination where things could not be touched or seen in the usual way. He was conscious of new questions which had to be brought under the control of his mind. He had to study himself and make clear his place in the universe. In this quest, such things as art, philosophy and religion developed.

Since man did not live by instinct, he had to work out his own rules for behavior. He had to develop his own set of personal values, which is called *morality,* and he had to devise a system of values for relations with other men, which is called *ethics.* Questions of ethics and morality confronted man from the beginning; they still do today.

This last element of culture, the use of mind and spirit, involves religion, ethics, art and morality—words which are not easily defined. We shall have to see man actually use these words, and we shall have to use them ourselves in order to understand them fully.

A few terms serve as keys for studying the various elements of culture, terms such as economics, politics, technology and ethics. A political study of culture will deal only with questions of leadership and government, whereas an economic study of culture will deal with such matters as trade, commerce and money. The anthropologist attempts to see culture as a whole, to understand why men in different cultures act the way they do. The historian also studies human culture as a whole, but in addition, he examines the *changes* made in culture during the passing of years and centuries. His approach is one of narration—he tells a story in which he traces the cultural evolution of man up to the present day. This is the method that we will use.

Define

anthropology
evolution
primates
hominids
homo sapiens

culture
economy
technology
linguistics
society

politics
morality
ethics
history

Review and Answer

1. What is the difference between physical and cultural anthropology? In what different ways would a physical anthropologist and a cultural anthropologist each go about his work?
2. How has the linguistic approach to human culture been used in this chapter?
3. What is the origin of the word "astronaut"? What does the choice of this word tell us about the origins of our own culture?
4. Give specific examples from modern society of (a) a political issue or problem, (b) an economic issue or problem, (c) a social issue or problem, and (d) a moral issue or problem.
5. What are the four elements of human culture? Can modern culture still be divided into these four elements?
6. Do you think that it is accurate to refer to man as a "naked ape"?

2

Paleolithic and Neolithic Culture

Just when the human primate developed a culture is difficult to pinpoint. However, human fossils and implements dating from about one million years ago have been found, indicating that man at that time was already a toolmaker. Man's cultural evolution began when the first "man" actually constructed such implements as scrapers or chisels from rough pieces of stone.

Most of our knowledge about early man and his culture is based on what we have learned from the tools which he made. Thus, stone tools have become the basis for dividing the history of early man into specific periods. The Greek word for stone is *eolith,* and the three prefixes *Paleo, Meso* and *Neo* mean respectively, old, middle and new. Combining these syllables gives us the words *Paleolithic, Mesolithic* and *Neolithic,* which identify the periods of man's early history, that is Old, Middle and New Stone ages.

Paleolithic Culture

Paleolithic culture began about one million years ago and lasted until about 10,000 B.C. This span of time comprises about 95 *percent of all human history!* In other words, almost all of human life was lived during the Old Stone Age when man was a hunter. All of the so-called improvements which we see around us today, therefore, have come about very recently.

Technology. Since the economic basis of Paleolithic culture was hunting, the technology of man in this society should be easy to deduce. The bow and arrow was perhaps the first complex machine invented by man; using this cultural creation multiplied his own strength. The discovery of how to kindle and control fire enabled man to live in cold climates, to cook food and, eventually, to smelt metals from rocks. Fire was the first source of energy harnessed by man which did not come from himself. It has remained the basic source of energy behind all of his future technology.

With the discovery of fire, nature was robbed, and some of its energy was placed at the disposal of man. It is no wonder that the legendary Greek hero Prometheus, who stole fire from the gods to give it to man, is such an important figure in the Greek myths.

Social Structure. The Paleolithic hunter had to follow the migrations of wildlife in order to keep the source of his food supply close at hand. Because a hunter must be constantly on the move, he develops no permanent settlements. All of the energies of the hunting group are directed toward the task of finding food. With no fixed home base, there was little permanence in the life of the Paleolithic hunter. Political organization was loose, with power and influence going to the most successful hunters. There was no private property, and no one individual could really go his own way; capturing and killing massive beasts required the total services of everyone. If, for any reason, the number of animals decreased, the population would decline; man was still at the mercy of nature.

Yet, in spite of what appears to be an extreme dependence on natural forces, Paleolithic man had created enough of a culture to make him superior to the animals. With the invention of tools such as the axe and weapons such as the bow and arrow, he had grasped the all-important principle that he could increase his power, not by depending on physical evolution, but by making things which could be detached from himself at will. An axe is, in a sense, an extension of a hand; man had made this extension and could use it in a number of ways rather than waiting for the development of an axe-like hand through an evolutionary process. Man was a toolmaker rather than a "toolgrower." Here we can see man's mind at work, grasping a principle.

Knowing that he was different from the animals, man became aware of nonanimal problems. Knowing now of sickness and death, man began to seek ways of dealing with the anxieties caused by this awareness; in the process, *magic* and *religion* had their origins.

Magic. Magic is one way of coping with certain kinds of human problems. It is a method by which man can control nature. Magic uses "supernatural" devices to gain specific ends. For example, during the Paleolithic period, if a man felt bad, he might consult the *shaman* (SHAH mun), who was an expert in the art of magic. The shaman, by performing a series of rituals and incantations, attempted to use nature to cure the man. Convinced that the magic was working and therefore relieved of anxiety, the man would sometimes appear to have been cured.

In another instance, a shaman might dress up as an animal and dance around, attempting to bring a real animal near enough to the camp to provide a target. Whether or not this magical activity actually did produce the animal, men were convinced that it did. In such a way, some anxiety was removed from their lives, and they felt more in control of the environment. Magic, therefore, was a practical operation designed to prevent something bad from happening or to cause something good to occur. Superstitious people today who carry rabbits' feet around are practicing a form of magic.

Religion. Religion is different from magic, and it forms a major part of man's culture even today. Unlike magic, religion was not used to gain immediate goals. Rather, it celebrated some important event or calmed some basic human fear. Religious activities grew up around significant events such as birth, coming of age, marriage or death. Religion also centered around the eating of food or the planting and harvesting of grain. In early times, religious ceremonies served the needs of society, giving members of a group a sense of

Dating from the Paleolithic age, this carved reindeer horn of a bison with turned head clearly shows early man's skill and sense of beauty.

Bulloz—Art Reference Bureau

unity and purpose. Therefore, religious leaders, sometimes called *priests,* were important members of a tribe. At important events in the life of an individual, a family or a tribe, man realized his separation from the harmony of nature; religion was a means of gaining a sense of security.

For example, when a young man became an adult, he went through a religious ceremony in which he was symbolically introduced to the values and beliefs of his tribe. This action helped to keep the society together and ensured the continuation of its values for the next generation. In primitive society, the horror of death and the fear of the dead body brought about the development of a ceremony of mourning and burial so as to keep the members of the tribe from going mad and possibly disrupting society. Paleolithic grave sites have been found in which bodies were buried in particular ways, often with implements next to them. This fact would seem to indicate that man believed in a life after death. Death was the most important problem which religion tried to explain, a problem with which religion still grapples.

The ceremonies accompanying the practice of religion were very important. Burial and the elaborate mourning ritual were designed to channel the emotion of grief in a nondestructive direction. The ceremonial eating of food served to infuse man's control of his environment with a religious importance. One Paleolithic religion was known as *totemism.* The *totem* was a particular animal, sacred to a given tribe, with which its members felt a strong relationship. In some cases, they believed that they were descended from this animal. In religious ceremonies, they often dressed in the skin of the animal and at times ate its flesh in order to gain some of its power and to establish communion with it. The lasting influence of this practice can be seen in the fact that some later religions retained the practice of a sacred meal. It also may be no accident that in medieval cathedrals, the four evangelists—Matthew, Mark, Luke and John—are often represented by animals.

As we shall see, when man developed civilization, his religion changed. The concept of gods was born, and religion was used by man to discover his place in the universe, to work out moral and ethical rules and to seek some purpose for his life. Man's religious quest is a major part of the history of civilization.

Since early man had no written language, it is impossible to know with certainty just what he was thinking about. In our study of early cultures, we must rely on things which man has made and which chance has allowed to remain. The study of such things is called *archaeology*, a science which deals with the material remains of man's culture. Telling what an entire culture was like from a collection of tools, trinkets and weapons is a difficult process involving a lot of guesswork and imagination. Yet, from what has remained of the distant Paleolithic period, it is apparent that, through tools, weapons and the ability to organize a hunt, man gained a dominant position in the animal world. The gradual growth in the quality and kinds of implements, such as fishhooks, needles and harpoons, shows that Paleolithic man was able to communicate his accomplishments to future generations.

Art. The most striking evidence of man's cultural achievement in the Old Stone Age is a collection of art works which, in the opinion of some experts, are the equal of work done in any period in man's history. Deep in the recesses of caves in Spain and southern France, archaeologists (scientists who specialize in archaeology) have discovered wall paintings, vivid in color and detail, painted by artists of the Paleolithic age. These paintings are of animals—as would be expected—and they represent not only man's ability to create works of beauty but also his ability to use his mind in an effort to control nature.

Many of the animals pictured in the wall paintings have arrows in them, which was man's way of killing the actual animal. He was trying to influence the world of reality through the use of imagination because, for him, there was no distinction between the world of art and the world of reality. Therefore, in these pictures, he was creating "real" things. By having pictures of animals in his caves, he could gain from them some of their power and also control their actions. These pictures clearly represent the development of religion and art in the culture of primitive man.

Paleolithic Man. During the long Paleolithic period (95 percent of man's life so far on earth), man created a culture which solved most of his problems. By modern standards, his life was short, brutal and uncertain. But Paleolithic man was able to cope with his environment for many thousands of years. Modern man, however, has lived with his for only a fraction of that time.

Paleolithic man's felling of large beasts, his taming of fire and his creation of graphic art show him to be a man of energy, intelligence and spirit. Since his culture is by far the greater part of our heritage, we may logically have some of his traits; the more we learn of the man of the Old Stone Age, the more we may learn of ourselves. His life was active, and his physical energies fully engaged. Our present culture is much more settled and less physically demanding. Yet, could it be that the wanderlust that man today often feels, the hunting instinct which drives men to the north woods and children on scavenger hunts and, above all, the seemingly endless desire of civilized man to hunt his fellowman in war merely show that there is something of Paleolithic man still evident in our culture?

In spite of the material and spiritual accomplishments of man in the Old Stone Age—and they were stupendous when contrasted with a society of chimpanzees—he was unable to advance beyond a certain point. With only a few exceptions, he had to remain entirely on the move. His food supply was irregular, and even if he became a more efficient hunter, there were just so many animals and no way to store and preserve the food. His numbers, therefore, remained small.

Scientists believe that there were about seven million people in the entire world during the Paleolithic period, fewer than there are in New York City today. If man had not developed the economic tools to alter radically his relationship to nature, we might still be as dependent on nature as Paleolithic man was. New inventions would not be enough. Better weapons would only make it possible to kill more animals than could be eaten at any one time, and so the basic supply of available food would be reduced. A fundamental change in man's relationship to nature had to occur in order to bring about a different pattern of life.

After the retreat of the last ice sheet (about 10,000 B.C.), we have evidence that some men began to rely less on animals and more on wild fruits and grains for their food. Some groups of people learned to "hunt" fish and therefore found it less necessary to migrate in search of food. Just why this gradual shift in the pattern of human life occurred is difficult to say. This period in which men led a more settled existence is called the *Mesolithic period* (Middle Stone Age); it lasted from about 10,000 to 6000 B.C. During this period, the pattern of climate became about what it is today in most of the world. Man was able to observe the regular pattern of the seasons with its effects on plant and animal life. The ability to remain relatively settled enabled man to take a different view of nature. It also prepared him for a cultural advance which was the most important achievement of all time, more important than the discoveries made in our own era.

Neolithic Culture

The Neolithic Revolution. The advance that would revolutionize man's way of life was made on the slopes of the hills in the southwestern portion of Asia, the area we call the Middle East, where the rains come in spring and winter on a fairly regular basis. In this area, some man, or perhaps a woman, noticed that when seed from ripened grain was dropped into the moist earth, something

Surviving Paleolithic art includes this primitive painting of a deer hunt, discovered in Los Caballos Cave in Spain.

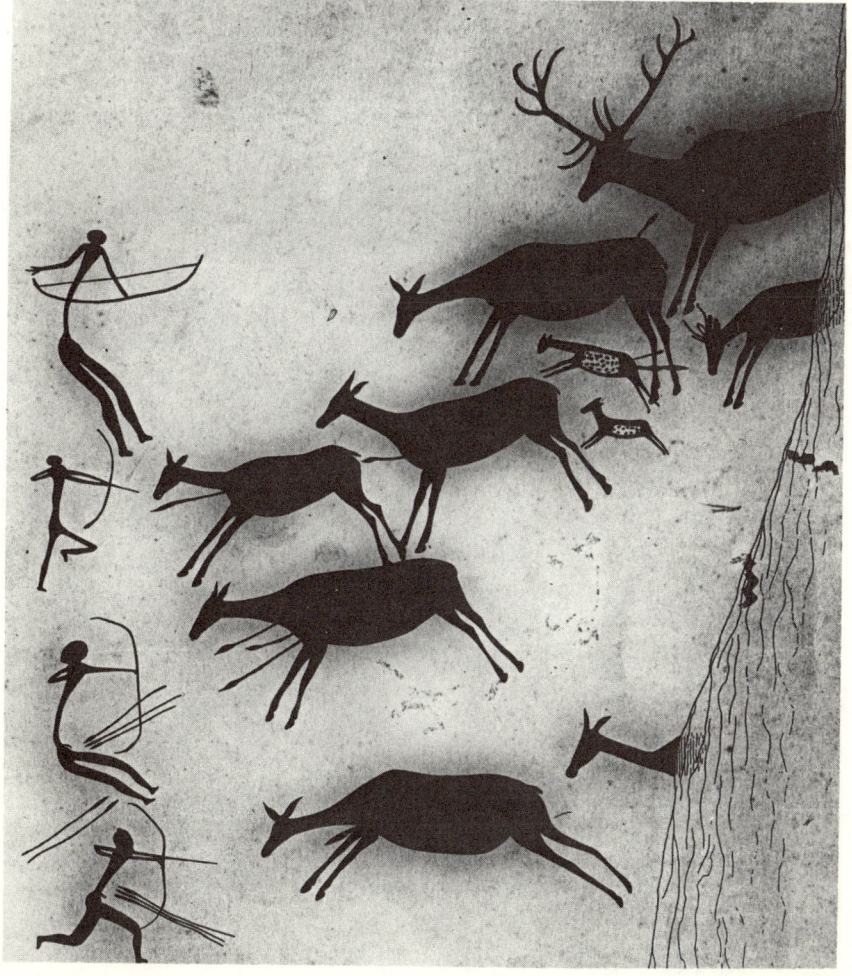

Mas—Art Reference Bureau

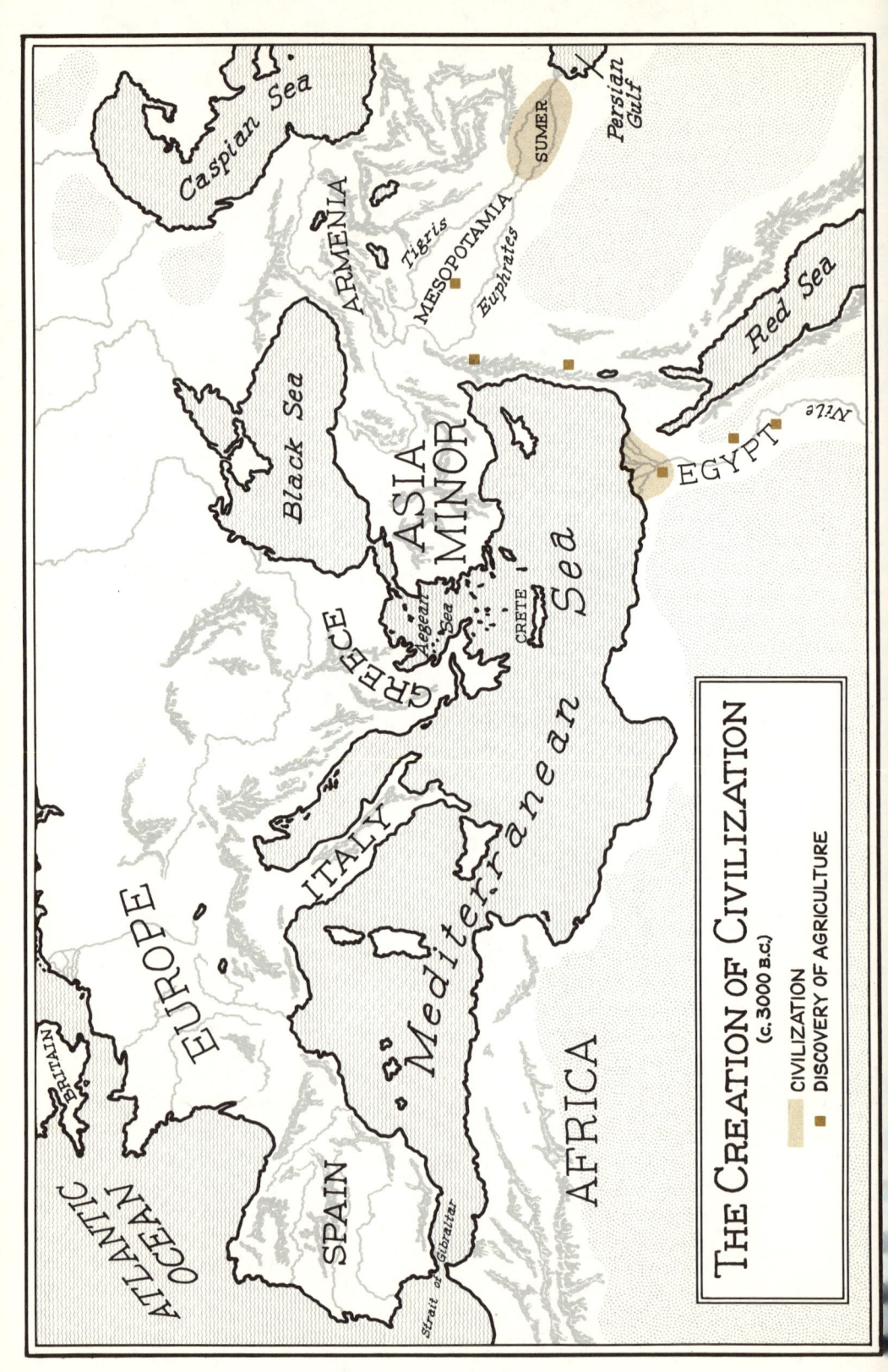

mysterious occurred. If one waited long enough, the seed produced new barley or wheat. If these seeds could be captured before falling to the ground, stored through the long dry summer and then planted, man could truly control his food supply and grow as much food as soil and rainfall would permit. So simple a thing as farming, developed about 6000 B.C. in the Middle East, was to change the entire future development of man.

Soon after the discovery of organized farming, man made another significant advance. He realized that some animals, captured and domesticated and fed the crops which he had grown, would reproduce in captivity and provide man with a permanent supply of meat, hides and milk. This twofold discovery, agriculture and the domestication of animals, ushered in what is called the *Neolithic period;* the discovery itself of farming and herding is called the *Neolithic Revolution.* These cultural advances revolutionized man's life because they put him in a totally different relationship to nature, one in which he used nature in a systematic way rather than occasionally looting it. He could now remain fixed in one place, he had additional leisure time during the growing season and he had ample food to increase his numbers.

Not only was this revolution a total change in the economic basis of human culture, but it was a rapid change as well. The discovery of farming and herding, which took a few thousand years to work itself out, might seem to us to be a slow change or evolution, but when we consider the fact that man had been living as a hunter for hundreds of thousands of years, a change which took place in a few thousand years is a rapid or revolutionary change. When looking at the whole period of man's existence on earth, the Neolithic Revolution happened only a short time ago, and the physical basis of our culture still rests on farming and domesticated animals.

A culture based on farming and herding, rather than on hunting, caused new problems and demanded new solutions. Because of the changed relationship between man and nature, human culture changed in some degree in everything—an agrarian economy affected all things, from the construction of tools to the development of religious ideas. We can mention only a few of the most important changes.

Beginning in Sumer and the Nile delta (as the map on page 20 shows), civilization spread along the river valleys and to the seacoast.

Technological Changes. The need to store grain and seed, and to cook the products of farming, led to the need for containers. This need, combined with the leisure time provided by the rhythm of farming, led to the discovery of pottery. Clay, if molded while moist, heated to a certain temperature and finally set off to cool, forms a hard substance which provides a heat-resistant container. To Neolithic man, the process of changing one substance into what seemed to be another must have been a magical operation. The experts in this craft, the potters, possessed an invaluable skill. The importance of the potter throughout the ancient world can be seen in the fact that ancient literature, especially Hebrew sacred writings, frequently uses the literary image of the potter working with his clay.

The step from working with clay to that of working with minerals was now an easy one, even though metallurgy is much more complex than clay work. Neolithic man discovered that copper ore, heated to the melting point, could be molded into any shape and made into implements for the cutting and working of certain types of stone. A broken copper tool or weapon could be refired and repaired or remolded. Copper, which produced superior tools and weapons, made the coppersmith a valuable person, so much so that he was relieved of routine work and supported by the rest of the tribe in return for his services. The coppersmith became a specialist, employing all his energies to develop and improve his one craft. The potential of metal was great. Since metal tools were needed to cut stone, large-scale architecture in stone could now come about. From these two advances in human technology, we can see how a change in conditions can lead to progress. The potter and the coppersmith could never have come about in Paleolithic culture.

Other achievements soon followed. The wheel, plow, loom, sail and building brick were all natural results of the kind of life lived in the Neolithic period. The discovery of metallurgy led to the development of bronze, a mixture (or alloy) of copper and tin, and later to the discovery of iron. Although it came late in the history of man, the Neolithic period is the bedrock of our modern culture; from discoveries made then, endless elaborations have evolved. Our culture will remain basically Neolithic in its relationship to nature until we develop the full-scale production of artificial food.

The importance of the Neolithic Revolution was expressed, perhaps unknowingly, by the American politician William Jennings Bryan more than seventy years ago when he said:

... the great cities rest upon our broad and fertile prairies. Burn down your cities and leave our farms, and your cities will spring up again as if by magic; but destroy our farms and the grass will grow in the streets of every city in the country.

Social Changes. Changes other than technological ones were also caused by the Neolithic Revolution. Farming required a settled life and caused an increase in population. With more people living in a small area, called a *village,* new problems of cooperation arose. Rules for holding and transferring property were now necessary, and some kind of government was needed to cope with the pressure of more people no longer on the move. Also, since good farming land was not found everywhere, there were probably conflicts between villages for the possession of land. Perhaps some of the energies which for so long had been used for the hunt were now channeled into war. In any event, improvement in some areas brought about new problems in cooperation.

What if two sons contested the right to their father's property? Who would decide the issue? What part of the land would be held by individuals, and what would be left for the whole community? Did the tools of the coppersmith belong to him and to his sons, or were they the property of all the villagers who had kept the smith alive? We have no record of Neolithic law or custom, but there must have been some unwritten system of law and justice on which everyone agreed. The problems of cooperation which arose at that distant time are still with us today in different forms, in both national and international affairs.

The Growth of Nature Religions. The rhythm of Neolithic life was quite different from that of Paleolithic life. Man had to rely on the changing seasons for his food rather than move in pursuit of it. The representation of animals in art largely vanished, and man's major anxiety focused on the soil and on the weather. Rain, sun, soil and seed were the keys to his life, and his religion reflected this change. The annual death and rebirth of nature brought about what we call *nature religions,* in which the various natural processes were worshipped. The earth was seen as the Earth Mother who nourished all life and brought forth food. This goddess is seen in many later religions under many forms. The theme of death and rebirth became, and in some cases still is, the basis of some aspects of religious life.

Neolithic man believed that the sky, sun, moon and rain were all controlled by supernatural powers beyond the understanding of man and that these powers had to be worshipped, flattered and sacrificed to. The focus of religion shifted from magical rocks and trees to major natural forces. During many thousands of seasonal changes, man developed an elaborate *mythology* (a collection of myths or stories dealing with the gods and legendary heroes of a people, usually involving supernatural elements) in an attempt to explain and, in part, to control the forces of nature on which human life depended.

Not all people became farmers. Some used domesticated animals as a source of food and moved each season with their herds to new grazing lands. This kind of life is called *pastoral,* from the Latin word *pastorem,* meaning shepherd. These people retained more of the traits of the Paleolithic period than did those who practiced only agriculture, and their interaction with agricultural people plays an important role in the history of man. The importance of pastoral life in the ancient world can be seen in the fact that many religious terms and symbols are drawn from the life of the shepherd. The very word pastoral has a religious significance, and in Hebrew and Christian thought, God himself is often likened to a shepherd.

To describe the nature of Neolithic culture in a few words would be difficult. Perhaps we can say that in general, the need for immediate gain, which was the dominant motive in a hunting society, disappeared, and a more relaxed and ordered kind of life took its place. This change took away the speed and vigor of a hunting life and channeled man's energies into new forms. The settled condition of Neolithic life led to a new pattern of inventions and the growth of certain specialized occupations. The Neolithic period also saw the birth of ideas which are found in some of the higher religions of today.

Yet the memory of an earlier way of life continued to haunt man, and perhaps still does. The nature of Neolithic life and the development of more social rules brought restrictions, and the freedom of the hunt was limited to meet the needs of farming. Many myths of the past idealize the pre-farming age of man and regard it as a kind of golden age when man was more a part of nature and not "over-civilized" with sets of rules and restrictions. In the Bible, the account of the Garden of Eden, where man lived in harmony with nature, is perhaps an example of this reference to an earlier, simpler and more natural life. Perhaps, then, for everything gained in human culture, there is something equally important lost. This feeling of alienation from nature was to increase when man took his next step and became "civilized."

Define

Paleolithic	totemism
Mesolithic	archaeology
Neolithic	nature religions
shaman	mythology
priest	pastoral

Review and Answer

1. What is the difference between magic and religion? Is the difference significant?
2. What was the Neolithic Revolution, and why can it be called a "revolution"?
3. Why could the potter and the coppersmith never have existed during the Paleolithic period of man's history?
4. How did man's pattern of life and view of the universe change when he entered the Neolithic period?
5. Do you think that it is significant that the Paleolithic period comprises 95 percent of all human history? Why or why not?
6. From what you know of the differences between the Paleolithic and Neolithic periods of history, do you think that it is wise to call them the "Old Stone Age" and the "New Stone Age"?

3

Civilization

Sometime between 6000 and 4000 B.C., farmers and herders, faced with exhausted soil and the pressure of population, moved into the valleys of two river systems: the Nile in North Africa and the Tigris and Euphrates in Southwest Asia. The rich soil deposited each year along the banks of these rivers, the constant supply of water and the marine life in the river itself provided an area which could support a large population. However, the area was marshy and thick with vegetation, and the rivers often flooded with great destructive force. If this area were to support a permanent society of humans, it would have to be cleared and drained, and the flooding of the river would have to be controlled by an elaborate irrigation system. The people who rose to this challenge, tamed the rivers and realized the potential of these two areas created what we call *civilization*. From the banks of the Nile and the Tigris and Euphrates, our present Western civilization has grown.

The Elements of Civilization

Once again, we are faced with a general word to be defined. Civilization is a special quality which some human cultures have developed, but once again, we must see what these cultures actually did before we can offer a general definition. What made the people who lived near the Nile, Tigris, and Euphrates rivers in the fourth millennium* B.C. civilized, and the people who did not live there uncivilized? Let us see, then, just what the river people did.

Intellectual Potential. First of all, the richness of the soil and the constant supply of water produced a surplus supply of food.

---

* A *millennium* is a period of a thousand years.

This economic fact represents a tremendous increase in the material side of culture. More people could be kept alive, and fewer people were needed to produce food. Population increased rapidly in these river valley areas, and more people were freed to use their minds rather than their hands.

A Written Language. Second, the task of organizing the control of the river, and the feeding and governing of many people compressed into a small area, caused many problems of communication and cooperation, problems which Neolithic man did not have to face. Just as the invention of pottery had been a response to a new problem, it might be said that the *invention of a written language* was the most important response to the needs of river people. The uses and consequences of a written language were tremendous. A class of people, usually called *scribes*, would develop the art of writing and would keep records. Wills, deeds, inventories and laws could all be written down, thereby permitting social and political organization to become more complex. Perhaps most important, the ideas of a man, once etched into clay or recorded on stone, could now have an influence beyond the man himself; ideas and knowledge could spread in both space and time. A thought could be written in one place and be read in many others in which the writer could not hope personally to appear in his lifetime; and the idea could have an influence long after the original thinker was dead. Ideas could have a life of their own, could become immortal, and more ideas could multiply with great rapidity.

The influence of a written language cannot be overemphasized; in fact, writing may be the one thing which makes a people civilized. Not only did it aid in the storing and spreading of knowledge, but it gave to man a new realm in which to express himself and to work out the creations of his mind and spirit. It gave him a new art form, literature, and in so doing, the minds of many men were stimulated. The great thinkers of the past, such as the Greek poet Homer, the Greek philosopher Socrates and the Hebrew religious and moral thinkers, including Jesus, did not themselves write down their thoughts. Yet written language kept their thoughts alive; through the written word, their ideas spread across the globe, giving shape and direction to later cultures, including our own.

Urbanization. Third, the people of these river valleys lived in cities, or what is called an *urban society*. Cities needed many kinds of people, such as scribes, metal workers, merchants, soldiers, servants and builders; the number of occupations grew as civilization

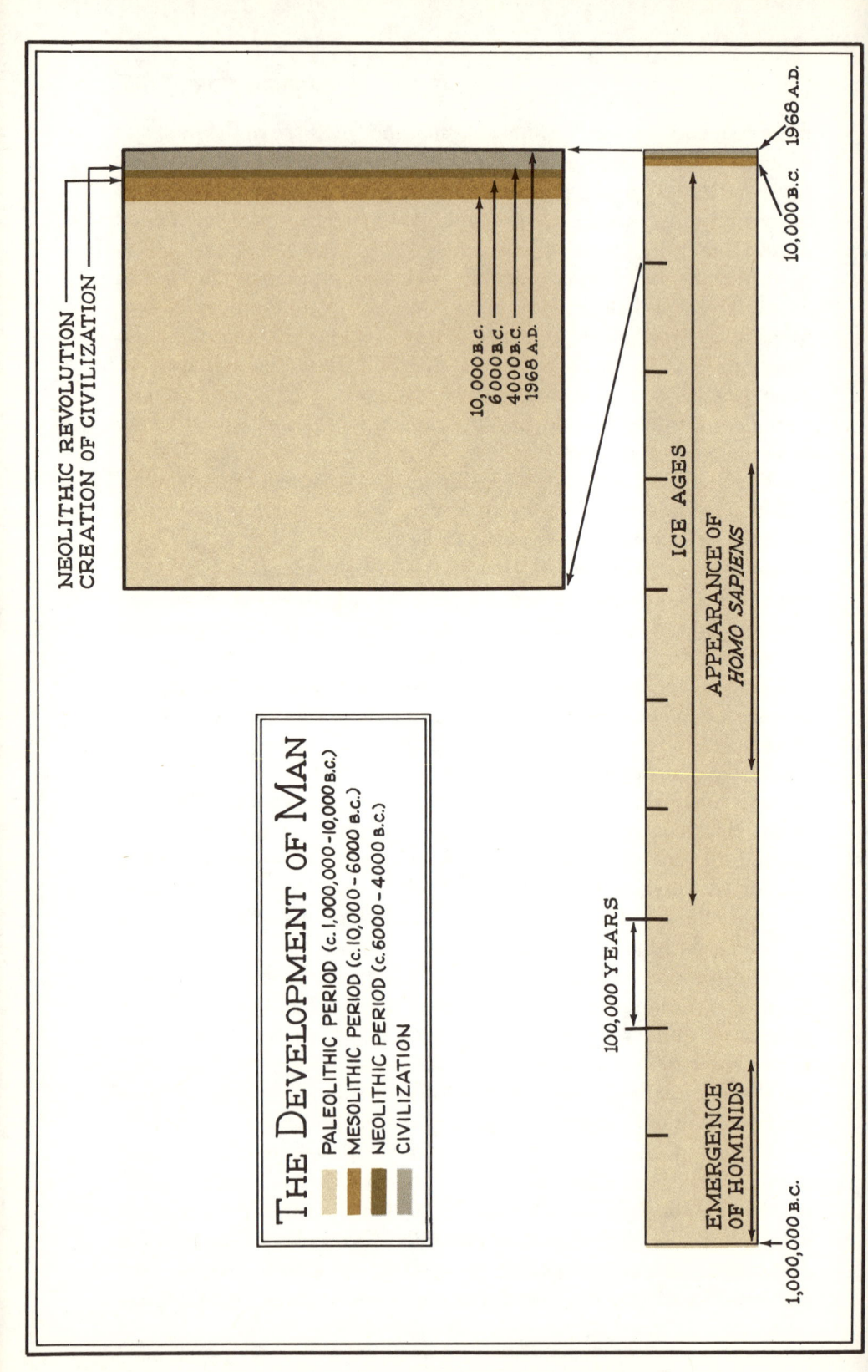

increased and spread. In the cities, there could be an increase in specialized labor skills, and the individual could have the opportunity to choose what he wanted to do to a far greater extent than he could have in either Paleolithic or Neolithic culture. Since fewer people were required to labor in the fields, some individuals could be free to go their own way and could undertake a variety of tasks. The degree of freedom of choice was small in early civilization, but freedom of choice was now possible for the first time. Civilization has always been associated with cities, and this is so even today. Perhaps there is a good reason why the word city is directly related to the word civilization.

Freed from a constant dependence on nature and the need to use all his energies to find food, man could begin to cultivate and develop his own nature. As he added more to his knowledge of the world and of himself and separated himself farther from nature, he was confronted with more problems concerning his nature and his destiny. In meeting some of these problems, the concept of religion was altered. Tribal rituals and a belief in vague powers of nature were no longer adequate for man's needs.

Civilized man was more conscious of his own personality than his ancestors had been. He therefore conceived of the forces of nature in personal terms; he developed the concept of gods, personal divine forces who were revealed in nature and who determined man's destiny. Religion, the belief in a reality unseen by man, had existed from man's earliest days. Civilization led to the idea of gods and mythology. Religion, therefore, existed before there were gods.

The Impact of Civilization

Five thousand years ago, the inhabitants of the Nile and Tigris-Euphrates valleys created some of the problems which we all face today—Who am I? Why was I created? How should I live my life? How should I treat my fellowman? Why must I die? The questions raised and the answers offered by these early people have been passed on through the ages, ultimately to all of us.

Most people tend to regard the progress from hominid to civilized man as a steady march of progress. Yet civilization is a mixed blessing. Such questions as "Who am I?" probably did not press upon uncivilized man the way they do on us. Civilization brought the distinction between rich and poor, slave and free, literate and illiterate. Organized wars and a sense of being alone in an uncon-

David Linton

The end of the Neolithic period saw the spread of a new idea: painted pottery. The pottery shown here dates from about 3500 B.C.

cerned universe are all products of civilization. Even the blessing of a written language can be seen as a mixed one. Man's memory became weaker. The story is told of a primitive man who watched an anthropologist taking notes. Struck by this strange practice, the native said, "What's the matter, can't you remember?"

Civilization is one of man's more recent creations. Man is thought to have emerged about 1,000,000 years ago; he discovered agriculture about 7,000 years ago; the first civilization was created as recently as 5,000 years ago. Considering the fact that man has lived about 95 percent of his existence without civilization, its creation was a revolution, a rapid thrusting of man into a new form of life. Perhaps this is why civilizations rise and fall, and why, at times, civilization itself seems in danger of destruction.

The power man gained in the Near East at the Nile, Tigris and Euphrates some 5,000 years ago has enabled him to create, invent and expand himself, perhaps too rapidly and beyond the bounds which nature has intended for him. One student of history, toying with the idea that the evolution of man might be "one of nature's extravagances," wrote:

> It has been suggested that the human brain is a kind of tumor, a monstrous overgrowth that has enabled him to indulge in biologically preposterous behavior, and that will eventually destroy him. Certainly he is now capable of self-destruction, as no other species is.

The conquest of civilization has brought man untold power, but time has yet to decide whether he has the strength to cope with his own creations.

This unit contains a number of generalizations and a discussion of "man" and "civilization." What follows in the rest of the book is a historical survey, a narration of specific things which specific men have done in one area of the world in the building of civilization. Some explanations will be offered as to why certain things have happened, but like humans in every age, we will have to come to grips with our own civilization. To do this, we must study the past, for to study history is to study ourselves. In this book, we will encounter the record of men, events and ideas. To each of them, we should ask three simple questions: What is it? Why is it? What of it?

Define

millennium
scribe
urban

Review and Answer

1. Why do you think that the creation of civilization took place where it did?
2. What does the word "civilization" as defined and used in this chapter mean?
3. What is "specialization"? Why is it significant in the history of man?
4. Why could the scribe never have existed in the Neolithic period?
5. Why was the development of a written language so important?
6. How did the creation of civilization affect man's relationship to nature and to his fellowman?

Reading 1

Mythological Thought

We live today in a scientific world. When we look at the physical world, we see it as a substance different and separate from us—a substance which we can understand by learning scientific laws, or as they were once called, "laws of nature." When snow melts, it forms water, which explains to our satisfaction why rivers tend to flood in the spring of each year. Diseases are caused by germs which can be seen and studied and whose actions scientists can sometimes predict. Even those parts of nature which are still mysteries to us are thought to follow regular patterns which we will eventually discover.

However, when we turn to *human* nature, it is difficult to develop laws. There is no fixed temperature of condensation for human emotion. When we cope with our fellow creatures, we use guess work and flattery; we learn to expect the unexpected because we are dealing with living persons. Ancient man, for the most part, regarded nature as we would regard other human beings. To the ancients, nature was not an inanimate substance, but the same substance as man, and as fully alive as he was. Ancient man did not have to personify the forces of nature; they were alive and personal to begin with. Rain, soil, disease and death were flattered, ordered about or pleaded with, just as we would deal with human beings.

As the forces of nature were alive, it was logical that man would tell stories about them rather than devise fixed laws. From this kind of activity, myth was born. We often tell about a person and so hope to explain his actions, or at times, we throw up our hands and exclaim that we don't know why he acted the way he did. For centuries, man threw up his hands in despair when confronted with the power of nature. When he began to develop a mythology, he took a massive step toward explaining and controlling that nature.

When a man drew a picture of a bison being killed by an arrow, he was not just representing that action—he was causing it actually to happen. There was no distinction between the animal he had drawn and the real animal; they were part of the same reality. A story is told of an American Indian who, after watching a white man draw pictures of buffalos, felt that he now knew why buffalos had decreased in number. The man had taken them and placed them in his book!

When ancient man enacted a religious ceremony celebrating the marriage of the king, he was not merely imitating the productive powers of nature—he was helping nature and actually causing it to rejuvenate itself to produce the harvest. The chemistry of the seed acting in the soil was unknown to him. The seed was a person in the hands of the

---

Adapted from Chapter I of Henri Frankfort, *et al.*, *The Intellectual Adventure of Ancient Man* (Chicago: The University of Chicago Press, 1946) by permission of The University of Chicago Press.

earth which was another person. Human nature and physical nature were seen as similar creations, and so what was true for man was true for the rest of nature. This was the origin of the mythological view of the universe. The expression "Mother Earth" was not just a figure of speech; it expressed reality.

As man's mental activity changed, nature became in his eyes less and less of a personal and living substance. Therefore, natural science took the place of myth, and human responses were not attributed to physical nature. This was a slow process, and even today, we sometimes speak in a mythological language. We say that the sun "rises" and "sets" when we know that it does not. When we say that "death laid his icy fingers on him," we are treating the absence of life as if it were a living substance. Our thinking may not be mythological, but our language, especially our poetry, is.

To the ancients, all thinking was mythological, and therefore a myth was an expression of truth as much as a scientific fact is to us. The ancient man merely had a different image or model of the world than we do. Today, when something happens in the physical world, we will ask "why"; ancient man would ask "who." The River Nile was worshipped in order to make it flood each year. Xerxes, a Persian king, whipped the sea when a storm once destroyed a bridge he was trying to build. The Egyptians acted out the daily birth of the sun in order to make it appear on the horizon. We no longer find it necessary to indulge in these kinds of actions, and to this extent, we perhaps have advanced beyond the ancients. We have a different image or model of the world.

Yet, we must do many things to keep from hurting one another's feelings and to cope with the delicate mechanism of human emotions. Thinking of human emotions as a "mechanism" might be an example of our own mythology. If future men discover scientific laws for human behavior, they well may laugh at the mythology of our social customs. Further advances in physical science may so alter our present image of the world that today's science may be tomorrow's mythology. Therefore, we must not regard the myths which we will read as being merely quaint stories. Just as our scientific knowledge is essential for our lives, the mythology of the ancients was essential for theirs. Many myths may be based on what we regard as an incorrect view of the facts, but they often contain great truths. One definition states that a myth is that which never happened but is always true.

In this unit, we will witness the creation of civilization. More precisely, we will present some specific facts about two specific civilizations which grew up in the Near East. There are two major river valleys in this area. One is formed by the River Nile in Egypt; the other lies between the Rivers Tigris and Euphrates in what is today the nation of Iraq. We will deal with the accomplishments of two peoples, the Sumerians and the Egyptians, and we will have an opportunity to compare the civilizations of each. We should also be able to come closer to understanding what civilization is.

UNIT II
The Creation of Civilization

4

Sumer

The Tigris and Euphrates rivers originate in the mountains of Armenia and flow southward, coming together and emptying into the Persian Gulf. The land between these two rivers is called *Mesopotamia*. The term Mesopotamia comes from two Greek words, both of which we have already met, and so we should be able to figure out what this new word means.

Near the mouth of the Tigris and Euphrates, the fertile land was occupied by a people called Sumerians, who made the land of Sumer what is believed to be the first civilized area in the world. Around the year 3000 B.C., the task of organizing society to drain the marshes and channel the water into irrigation ditches was completed. It is from this time that written documents have been found enabling us, for the first time, to know what man was really thinking about.

The Sumerians, the first people to dwell in cities, moved into Mesopotamia from the north. Their civilization was to last for about one thousand years until they were invaded and conquered. The land has no natural boundaries such as mountains; thus, over the centuries, it was subject to frequent migrations and invasions. Yet throughout the entire history of Mesopotamia, no matter what kind of people were living there, the basic forms of civilization—styles of religion, mythology and art—followed the pattern established by the Sumerians. This situation is somewhat like that of the United States, where the basic culture is English even though millions of non-English people have moved there. In both the United States and Mesopotamia, changes occurred, but the fundamental forms of civilization remained constant.

Geographical Features

Nature offered much to the people of Sumer, but only with certain serious drawbacks. The riverbed was high and the Sumerian plain low, making flash floods a common occurrence. In addition, blinding winds often swept in off the surrounding desert, and destructive tropical storms blew in from the Persian Gulf. About 150 years ago, in fact, in 1831, the Tigris is reported to have flooded and destroyed seven thousand homes in a single night! Sumerian culture was influenced by these geographical features, and it is a striking example of the power of man that he was able to develop a government, a legal system and a rich literature in an area which offered so much to man but at the same time demanded so much of his energies.

Social and Political Structure

The City-state. Although flooding was irregular, the rivers tended to rise in the spring of each year. Unless meticulous and constant care was given to the process of irrigation, either too much water or stagnant pools would result. Along the river, people grouped together in small units whose major task was the regulation of the water supply. These small units grew into political organizations, and eventually, Sumer was dotted with a large number of small, separate states, often called *city-states*. Therefore, although we can speak of a Sumerian civilization, we cannot speak of a Sumerian nation. (The situation is comparable to Latin America today where there is a single Latin American culture, but many Latin American nations.) A good deal of warfare existed among the Sumerian city-states, and even though one or another state ruled the rest for a short period of time, the entire area was not politically unified.

The only major buildings which archaeologists have found in Sumer are the ruins of temples. The Sumerians took great pains to please the gods and see that they were properly worshipped—probably because the destruction of cities by either nature or human warfare was a fairly common occurrence. Their temples were high buildings called *ziggurats*, each with a terraced tower at the top. The Sumerian temple was more than just a church; it served as a place of food storage, a political headquarters and a house for keeping records.

Government. All land was believed to be owned by the gods, a belief which explains the central position of the temple and the importance of the priests in Sumerian society. Later in the history of Sumer, kings came to rule, but even they were servants of the gods, and the priests retained a good deal of importance. Religion was an essential part of Sumerian life and culture. This kind of government, in which the religious leaders are also the political leaders, is called a *theocracy*. The uncertainty of Sumerian life made the people dependent on their gods and led them, as well as the later inhabitants of Mesopotamia, to develop an elaborate religious system and a powerful religious literature and mythology.

The Development of Specialization and Trade. Mesopotamia, although rich in its soil, was poor in mineral resources. Since metal is an important element of civilization, it had to be brought into the land of Sumer. That trade existed can be proved by the remains of metal products found in Sumerian ruins. Trade requires merchants, and an important merchant class is a noticeable element in Mesopotamian society. The mountains to the east and north of Sumer were rich in minerals and timber, and merchants could exchange both food and finished metal products such as cups and weapons for these raw materials. Traveling merchants spread the arts of civilization and exposed the Sumerians to the influence of other peoples. The merchant is a good example of a specialist, a person freed from the burden of farming to follow another occupation. The surplus food supply produced by the fertile soil in Sumer made such specialists possible.

In Sumer, then, we can see a well-developed society with a number of people employed in specialized crafts. Most men lived as farmers, but there had to be craftsmen to make tools and to provide the products with which to trade, merchants to carry the products, scribes to keep records, priests to handle the all-important worship of the gods and administrators to see to the maintenance of irrigation dams and ditches.

Cultural Features

A written language was essential for this complex kind of life, and it is also essential for our knowledge of this civilization. If the Sumerians had not written down what they were thinking about, we would have to base our knowledge of them on archaeological remains alone. This would provide an incomplete picture. What, for example, would future generations make of our civilization from looking at some ruined buildings, a baseball bat and a television set?

A Written Language. Sumerian writing was called *cuneiform*, and this style of writing was to remain the method of written expression in Mesopotamia for centuries. No alphabet was used; rather, symbols standing for words or syllables were impressed by a wedge-shaped pen into a piece of soft clay. When the clay was baked, it became a hard tablet; these tablets were Sumerian books. Since each word or syllable had to have a different symbol, cuneiform writing, or for that matter any non-alphabetic writing, is a difficult thing to learn. Many years were spent in the task of learning to write, and the scribe was a distinctive and important person in society. A glimpse into the process of education can be seen in a fragment of a story written about a Sumerian schoolboy, who says:

> I went to school. . . . I recited my tablet, ate my lunch, prepared my new tablet, wrote it, finished it. . . . Then they assigned me my written work. When school was dismissed, I went home, entered my house and found my father sitting there. I told my father of my written work, then recited my tablet to him, and my father was delighted.

This story shows not only that education in Sumer involved a good deal of learning by copying and repetition, but it represents the first real individual person we have seen in the long history of mankind. Even though this boy is nameless, the long silence of the Paleolithic and Neolithic periods is here broken, and we can hear people who are recognizable as fellow humans.

As the story continues, it seems that the student was not perfect. His "hand copy was not satisfactory," and he was caned by the teacher. The boy's father then invited the teacher to dinner and gave him the best food and drink he had. Treated in such a fashion, the teacher then said:

> Young man, because you did not neglect my word, did not forsake it, may you reach the pinnacle of the scribal art, may you achieve it completely. . . . Of your brothers may you be their leader, of your friends may you be their chief, may you rank the highest of the schoolboys. . . . You have carried out well the school's activities, you have become a man of learning.

Just how true the well-fed teacher's words were is open to question. Nonetheless, we can see here an important consequence of the literacy which civilization had produced. By knowing how to write, the boy would gain a higher place in society and would have more prestige and power than those who were not "men of learning." Civilization did much to separate men from each other and to place them in different classes. From this development, progress resulted, but along with it came the separation of man from man through a process of distinction.

Literature. Most of the tablets from Sumer which archaeologists have found are merely lists of food supplies stored in temples. But some, like the story of the schoolboy, show the beginnings of

Scholars have identified over five hundred cuneiform symbols, each of which stands for a word or group of words in Sumerian writing.

a literature. One literary form which was created by the Sumerians was that of the *lament* or *lamentation,* which was used to express grief in the face of disaster. The two laments which follow will involve us directly in the heart of the first civilization. The first one mourns the destruction of the city of Ur (located in present-day Iraq). It concerns Enlil, the god of the air and storm.*

> Enlil called the storm.
> > The people mourn.
> Exhilarating winds he took from the land.
> > The people mourn.
> Good winds he took away from Sumer.
> > The people mourn.
> He summoned evil winds.
> > The people mourn.
> Entrusted them to Kingalunda, tender of storm.
>
> He called the storm that will annihilate the land.
> > The people mourn.
> He called the disastrous winds.
> > The people mourn.
> Enlil—choosing Gibil as his helper—
> Called the (great) hurricane of heaven.
> > The people mourn.
>
> The (blinding) hurricane howling across the skies,
> > —The people mourn.—
> The shattering storm roaring across the land,
> > —The people mourn.—
> The tempest which, relentless as a flood wave,
> Beats down upon, devours the city's ships,
> All these he gathered at the base of Heaven.
> > The people mourn.
>
> (Great) fires he lit that heralded the storm.
> > The people mourn.
> And lit on either flank of furious winds
> > The searing heat of desert.
> Like flaming heat of noon this fire scorched.

This was no doubt a public lament in which the worshippers responded with "the people mourn" after each line of the poem.

The second lament is of a more personal nature and is placed in the mouth of a goddess as she grieves over the destruction of her city.

> In the rivers of my city dust has gathered, truly
> > they have been made into fox dens;

---

* In all quotations throughout the book, words in parentheses indicate a conjecture made by the translator when the meaning in the original was unclear or unknown.

>   In their midst the foaming waters no more flow,
>   the workmen have deserted them;
>   In the fields of the city there is no more grain
>   the farmer has departed...
>   My palm-groves and vineyards that abounded with honey
>   and wine have brought forth the mountain thorn...
>   Woe is me, my house is a ruined stable,
>   I am a herdsman whose cows have been scattered,
>   I ... like an unworthy shepherd on whose flock
>   the weapon has fallen.
>   Woe is me, I am an exile from the city that has
>   found no rest.
>   I am a stranger dwelling in a strange city.

Reading these two pieces of literature should help us to sense both the uncertainty of Sumerian life and the strength of their religious expression. Much of the tone and imagery of these laments has had an influence upon later civilizations, and that influence can be clearly seen in the literature of the ancient Hebrews. A line-by-line reading of these poems can tell us much about many aspects of Sumerian culture as well as about their religion.

Religious Beliefs

Perhaps we can learn the most about an early civilization from a study of the religion in which all its people believed. Remember that as man separated himself from nature by becoming civilized, he had to explain his relationship to nature and his place in the scheme of things. To this end, the Sumerians had many gods who did and said many things, often acting as distant, superhuman and immortal men, beings moving in mythic form through a pulsating and alive nature. Their actions caused things to happen in the world, and the Sumerians described their gods in forms which they knew best—human forms.

A large collection of gods, representing certain forces of nature but usually taking human form rather than remaining as vague impersonal forces, is called a *pantheon*. The Sumerian pantheon was elaborated in a complete mythology similar in some ways to that which the Greeks would use in later times to describe their pantheon.

Sumerian Cosmology and Mythology. Any system of thought which claims to explain the nature of the universe is called a *cosmology, cosmos* being the Greek word for universe and *logia* meaning knowledge of. As we might expect, Sumerian cosmology was totally mythological in its form. The sky, which was the most imposing and permanent of natural wonders, was *Anu* (AH noo). *Enlil* was the god of the air and storm. *Enki* (EN kee) was the god of water from which all fertility and life sprang, and *Inanna* (ee NAH nah) was the goddess of the earth, the mother of all. There were, of course, lesser spirits and demons because all of nature was filled with gods—the sun, moon, major stars and planets and even such things as plants, reeds and salt. Certain cities had their own particular gods, but Anu, Enlil, Enki and Inanna were the cosmic gods who were everywhere.

In Sumer, the economic basis of society was agriculture. The following short mythological tale shows how the goddess Inanna expressed her approval of farming as a way of life. In the myth, a farmer and the shepherd Dumuzi both seek the favor of the goddess. The sun god speaks to Inanna, saying:

> O my sister, the much possessing shepherd,
> O maid Inanna, why dost thou not favor?
> His oil is good, his date-wine is good,
> The shepherd, everything his hand touches is bright,
> O Inanna, the much possessing Dumuzi,
> Full of jewels and precious stones,
> Why dost thou not favor?

Inanna answers:

> The much-possessing shepherd I shall not marry,
> In his new . . . I shall not walk,
> In his new . . . I shall utter no praise,
> I, the maid, the farmer I shall marry,
> The farmer who makes plants grow abundantly,
> The farmer who makes the grain grow abundantly.

In order to explain where the moon came from, the Sumerian cosmology held that it had materialized out of the atmosphere; in mythological terms, the moon was the child of the god of the air. Since nature was human, the following myth developed about Enlil, the god of the air.

> One day Enlil sees a young girl bathing in a stream. The girl eventually becomes the mother of Enlil's child. The child she bears is the moon god. The rest of the gods are outraged at Enlil's action and banish him to the underworld, the dark land of the dead where there is little joy. Enlil lives with the girl and becomes the father of three more children who become the gods of the underworld. Finally, by the intervention of the high gods, Enlil is called back to heaven and the young girl is forgotten.

What does this myth mean? The fate of the girl might well give us some indication as to the Sumerian opinion of women! In addition, the myth not only described the creation of the moon from the air but also expressed the good and bad side of Enlil, who was the god of the wind and air, as well as the god of the storm and hurricane. His twofold nature is made clear by seeing him as the father of not only the moon god, but of the gods of the underworld as well. Enlil is here portrayed as a rather headstrong and not too moral person, but this is how the weather often appeared to the Sumerians. The myth therefore conformed with reality.

Another Sumerian myth dealt with man's imperfections and the suffering he had to endure.

> One day when the gods were drinking too much, Enki challenged the earth goddess to make deformed men out of clay. He would then try to find some use for them. Among the imperfect creations were a man and a woman who could have no children. In triumph, Enki made the man a keeper of a harem and the woman a lady in waiting in the royal court. Now it was his turn. He made a perpetually blind person and a man who was so continually old that he could not feed himself. The earth goddess thought and thought, but she could find no use for these creatures. The gods laughed at her defeat in the game and returned to their pleasures.

Faced with human imperfection, sickness and old age as realities in the world, the Sumerians believed that this was how these things originated—they were created when the gods were drunk and playing games with each other, using humans as toys. Later cultures coped differently with this problem, but even today, man has not yet provided any generally acceptable explanation for imperfection and suffering in the world. The great gulf between the world of the gods and that of men as portrayed in the myth of Enki and the earth goddess should be painfully noticeable to the modern reader. Progress in religious thought might well be seen as an attempt to bridge this gap and to provide better answers to human problems.

The "Righteous Sufferer" Prayer. Sumerian religion did not contain any developed concept of an after-life. This lack led to a good deal of anxiety and some serious moral problems. People can bear much in life if they can look forward to some kind of judgment after death in which the good man is rewarded and the wicked man punished. Some cultures had within their religious systems a belief in the immortality of the human soul, and some did not. Some,

Survivors from Sumer's past, these alabaster statuettes are over four thousand years old. The beardless man in front may be a priest, and the two tallest figures, a god and goddess. The others are worshippers. Their expressions reflect the quality of Sumerian civilization.

like the Sumerians, did not even have the concept of a soul. The following selection is a prayer or petition directed by a righteous and religious man to his god. He has done all that his religion requires of him, and he says:

> ... I have become like a deaf man.
> Once I behaved like a lord, now I have become a slave...
> The fury of my companions destroys me.
> The day is sighing, the night is weeping;
> The month is silence, mourning is the year.
>
> I have arrived, I have passed beyond life's span.
> I look about me: evil upon evil!
> My affliction increases, right I cannot find.
> I implored the god, but he did not turn his countenance;
> I prayed to my goddess, but she did not raise her head.
>
> When come the evil things everywhere?
> I looked backwards; persecution, woe!
>
> Yet I myself was thinking only of prayer and supplication:
> Supplication was my concern, sacrifice my rule;

> The day of the worship of the gods was my delight,
> The day of the goddess' procession was my profit and wealth.
> Veneration of the king was my joy,
> And I enjoyed music in his honor.
> I taught my land to observe the divine ordinances,
> To honor the name of the goddess I instructed my people.
>
> The king's majesty I equated to that of a god,
> And reverence for the royal palace I inculcated in
>   the troops.
> Oh that I only knew that these things are well pleasing
>   to a god!
> What is good in one's sight is evil for a god.
> What is bad in one's own mind is good for his god.
> Who can understand the counsel of the gods in the midst
>   of heaven?
> The plan of a god is deep waters, who can comprehend it?
> Where has befuddled mankind ever learned what a god's
>   conduct is?
> He who was loving yesterday has died today:
> Instantly he is made gloomy, suddenly he is crushed.
> One moment he sings a happy song,
> And in an instant he will moan like a mourner.
> Like day and night their mood changes.
> When they are hungry they resemble corpses,
> When they are sated they rival their god;
> In good luck they speak of ascending to heaven,
> When they are afflicted they grumble about going down to
>   the underworld.

This is a remarkable piece of writing. It shows the thoughts of a sensitive and civilized man set free from a dependence on nature but standing alone in a universe which seems to have no sense to it. He lists his good actions; he has been a good man, but still misfortune follows him. He knows that the gods control both the universe and his destiny, but he is unable to understand them. "Where has befuddled mankind ever learned what a god's conduct is?" He puts his finger on the anguish of the human condition. At times, man understands his condition and is almost like god. But then, in a moment, he is no better than a beast, beset by uncertainty.

We should note that the prayer just quoted is the outcry of an individual man, set apart from his fellowman, trying to discover the ways of the gods and to seek justice for himself. The problem of justice—the difference between things which are fair and those which are unfair—was one of the problems caused by civilization. This man can be seen as a "Righteous Sufferer," a good man who suffers for no just reason. Much time and energy is spent by civilized man attempting to seek an answer to the problem of justice.

Sumerian Writings

Not all problems facing the Sumerians were as profound as those of the "Righteous Sufferer"—a man with a religious and moral dilemma. There were also less demanding issues.

Social Problems. The creation of civilization made possible education and leisure time, at least for some people. This advance brought with it its own set of problems. In the following story, discovered on a cuneiform tablet, a Sumerian father is dealing with what could be called a social problem. The father is angered with his son, for reasons which will become clear, and says to him:

> "Where did you go?"
> "I did not go anywhere."
> "If you did not go anywhere, why do you idle about? Go to school, stand before your 'school father,' recite your assignment, open your schoolbag, write your tablet, let your 'big brother' write your new tablet for you. After you have finished your assignment and reported to your monitor, come to me, and do not wander about in the street. Come now, do you know what I said?"
> "I know, I'll tell it to you."
> "Come now, repeat it to me."
> "I'll repeat it to you."
> "Tell it to me."
> "Come on, tell it to me."
> "You told me to go to school, recite my assignment, open my schoolbag, write my tablet, while my 'big brother' is to write my new tablet. After finishing my assignment, I am to proceed to my work and to come to you after I have reported to my monitor. That's what you told me."
> "Come now, be a man. Don't stand about in the public square, or wander about the boulevard. When walking in the street, don't look all around. Be humble and show fear before your monitor. When you show terror, the monitor will like you.
> "You wander about in the public square, would you achieve success? Then seek out the first generations. Go to school, it will be of benefit to you. My son, seek out the first generations, inquire of them.
> "What I am about to relate to you turns the fool into a wise man, holds the snake as if by charms, and will not let you accept false phrases. Because my heart had been sated with weariness of you, I kept away from you and heeded not your fears and grumblings—no, I heed not your fears and grumblings. Because of

your clamorings, yes because of your clamorings—I was angry with you—yes, I was angry with you. Because you did not look to your humanity, my heart was carried off as if by an evil wind. Your grumblings have put an end to me, you have brought me to the point of death.

"I, never in all my life did I make you carry reeds to the cane-brake. The reed rushes which the young and the little carry you, never in your life did you carry them. I never said to you, 'follow my caravans.' I never sent you to work, to plow my field. I never sent you to work, to dig up my field. I never sent you to work as a laborer. 'Go, work and support me,' I never in my life said to you.

"Others like you support their parents by working. If you spoke to your kin, and appreciated them, you would emulate them. They provide 72 bushels barley each—even the young ones provided their fathers with 72 bushels each. They multiplied barley for their father, maintained him in barley, oil, and wool. But you, you're a man when it comes to perverseness, but compared to them you are not a man at all. You certainly don't labor like them—they are the sons of fathers who make their sons labor, but me—I didn't make you work like them.

"I, night and day am I tortured because of you. Night and day you waste in pleasures. You have accumulated much wealth, have expanded far and wide, have become fat, big, broad, powerful, and puffed. But your kin waits expectantly for your misfortune, and will rejoice at it because you looked not to your humanity."

An idle son who refused to do what his father wanted him to do could not have existed in the Paleolithic or even in the Neolithic age. The surplus food produced by Sumerian technology made possible great progress but at the same time produced social problems such as the one we have just read about. From the time of the Sumerians, fathers have been perplexed by the actions of sons who have the education and leisure time to break out and follow their own paths.

Proverbs. Even though we may think that the Sumerians were gloomy people, fearful of the gods and pessimistic about the capabilities of man, they had many qualities which have a modern ring to them. Consider the following proverbs which were written by an unknown Sumerian scribe.

> He has not supported a wife or a child,
> His nose has not borne a leash.
>
> I am a thoroughbred steed
> But I am hitched to a mule
> And I must draw a cart
> And carry reeds and stubble.

> Who is well provided, who is rich?
> For whom shall I hold my love?
>
> Upon my escaping from the wild ox,
> The wild cow confronted me.
>
> Friendship lasts for a day
> Kinship endures forever.

Some of these sayings might be translated into modern terms carrying the same meaning.

Sumerian Society—an Overview

When we look at the entire picture, Sumerian society and its view of the world was really quite different from ours. In spite of the existence of trade and industry, agriculture was the basis of society, and most people worked in the fields from dawn to dusk. All of society was ordered in a *hierarchy* (a system of ranks of power and status) which seldom changed. Although the rule of the priests in the temple community gave way to the power of kings, there is no record of any attempt made to change the basic structure of society. Even the merchants who moved about and had a good deal of freedom apparently were not dissatisfied with the government and never organized themselves to resist it, be it one of priests or kings. The structure of society had been instituted by the gods, and it was man's task to accept the system as it was, pleading with the divine powers to make his lot as pleasant as possible. We have no record of an organized revolution throughout the entire history of Sumer. Perhaps the people were content. The need to gain security from starvation or attack, let alone to produce the wealth needed to sustain civilization, led to the acceptance of a rigid social system in which each man performed his chosen task and bowed to the will of the gods.

The striking difference between us and the Sumerians was vividly seen when some royal graves in the city of Ur were opened by the famous English archaeologist, Sir C. Leonard Woolley. In these tombs were found the bodies of a king and queen along with those of their courtiers and horses. The circumstances of the burial were remarkable.

> Woolley concluded that these men and women—who from their dress and ornaments were not mere slaves—had walked down the ramp into the pit, lain down and taken poison or perhaps a drug such as opium or hashish, which would have rendered them

Art Reference Bureau, British Museum

This mosaic of engraved shell and lapis lazuli from Ur depicts Sumerian royalty in times of peace. The top panel shows the king, his officers and two entertainers. In the bottom panel, various animals are being led—and all are probably destined for the banquet table.

unconscious. The wagons would have to be backed down the ramp, the animals slain, after which the groom and riders also took poison. One can imagine the solemn rites which would accompany such a burial, the chanting, the prayers and offerings. For a brief time the rows of bodies, in their bright costumes, the gold and silver of their ornaments gleaming in the sun, would lie open to the sky. Then at last the earth thudded down on them, sealing them from sight for five thousand years.

And these were not mere crumbling skeletons surrounded by a handful of barbaric ornaments, but the richly clothed bodies of kings, queens and their attendants; there were helmets and crowns of gold, golden drinking-cups, statues, ornaments of silver, a harp of gold and mosaic, an inlaid gaming board. But there was something else. As these fragile things were gradually brought to light by the patient hands of the archaeologists, they told a story which was both horrible and magnificent. It revealed, among those ancient people, a depth of faith—or of credulity—which to us is inconceivable; and also perhaps a degree of courage which few of us can imagine, let alone attain. For a brief moment human beings of the 20th Century A.D. came into contact with those of the 20th Century B.C. and found that contrary to sentimental assumptions they were not "just like us."

The physical contents of these tombs can tell us much about the art and wealth of the Sumerians, but the human remains should serve to remind us of the infinite variety of human civilization. In this burial, we see a creation of man's culture, a set of values and beliefs which compelled men to employ their wealth, energies and even their lives in the service of a religious ideal. We may think that we have improved since those days because we would not waste men and materials to such an end. But this royal burial was a meaningful action to the Sumerians, and it well may be that people of a future civilization will look at many of our most important and meaningful actions and regard them as equally futile and senseless.

Man remains the same. Many things which the Sumerians did we would do also. Some of the problems which they faced confront us as well. However, their civilization had a different shape than ours, and as a result, they saw themselves and the world in a very different light than we do. As the Sumerians were different from us, they were different also from another people who were building their own civilization in the Near East, the Egyptians, whom we will study in the next chapter.

Define

theocracy
cuneiform
pantheon

cosmology
hierarchy

Review and Answer

1. Find out the origins of each of the words listed above. What do these origins tell us about our own culture in which these words are used?
2. What do the examples of Sumerian mythology given in the text tell us about the Sumerians' concept of man, nature and the gods, and the relationship among them?
3. Write a modern version of the discussion between the Sumerian schoolboy and his father.
4. What is the problem faced by the "Righteous Sufferer"? Does this problem exist today?
5. If you were to write an economic, social and political history of Sumer, what facts would you include for each topic?

5

Egypt

The Sumerians began building a civilization a short time before the year 3000 B.C. Slightly later, the inhabitants of North Africa, when faced with decreasing rainfall, moved close to the River Nile and began a similar process. Egypt is the second source of civilization in the Near East.

Geographical Features

The River Nile. The Nile has its source in the mountains of Ethiopia and flows north to the Mediterranean Sea through fifteen hundred miles of desert and over five cataracts, or waterfalls. As the river approaches the sea, the lack of any tides or currents permits a continual depositing of silt, which forms a delta of rich soil. This process is still going on today. In the fall of each year, rainfall near the source of the Nile causes it to rise and overflow its banks, thereby spreading a layer of fertile soil on the arid desert near the river. The Nile rises only once a year at the same time, and since its riverbed is low, the flooding is usually rather mild. Because there is no rainfall in the area, the Nile is the only source of water, and therefore the sole source of life. Egypt *is* the Nile. It is an elongated oasis surrounded on both sides by trackless desert.

In modern Egypt, only 3.5 percent of the land is arable, and 99.5 percent of the population lives on this fertile strip. People who wander too far into the desert can easily be killed by the intense heat. The ancient Greeks called the land "the gift of the Nile," and this description is true even today. The Nile is so essential to an understanding of Egypt, and is so much a part of the rhythm of its society, that its importance cannot be emphasized too much. The following description of the river should be read with great care and imagination.

> In the summer the river lies quiet and slow between its shrunken banks, while the fields beside it parch and turn to dust and blow away toward the desert. Unless water can be raised by a series of lifts from the river or from very deep wells, agricultural growth comes to a standstill, and people and cattle grow thin and torpidly look upon the face of famine.
>
> Then, just as life is at its lowest ebb, the Nile River stirs sluggishly and shows a pulse of power. Through the summer it swells slowly but with increasing momentum until it begins to race with mighty waters, burst its banks, and rush over the miles of flat land lying on each side. Great stretches of moving muddy water cover the land. In a year of a high Nile they encroach upon the little mud-brick houses, and bring some of them tumbling down. From inert, dusty wastes, the land has turned to a great shallow stream, which carries a refertilizing load of silt. Then the peak of the flood passes, and the waters become more sluggish. Out of the flooded stretches there appear little peaks of soil, refreshed with new fertile mud. The torper of men disappears; they wade out into the thick mud and begin eagerly sowing their first crop of clover or grain. Life has come again to Egypt. Soon a broad green carpet of growing fields will complete the annual miracle of the conquest of life over death.

Even though in ancient Egypt the river was a gentle source of life, a tremendous amount of organization was necessary to cope with the annual flooding. The water had to be channeled and stored so that all possible land could be irrigated for the longest period possible. Property had to be surveyed and records kept so that when the water receded, there would be no question as to who owned what land. Preparation also had to be made for those years when the floods were lower than usual. One of the dangers of living in a very fertile area is that in prosperous times, a large population usually grows up, which is then in danger of starvation in the event of a bad year. The fact that during times of famine, other nations traded with Egypt for food indicates that the Egyptians must have developed an extraordinary kind of social and political system in order to control the forces of nature to such a degree.

An Isolated Land. The political stability of Egypt may be attributed in part to geographical factors. The valley of the Nile is surrounded on each side by hundreds of miles of desert. Invasion or migration was difficult at best, and, except for the narrow Isthmus of Suez, which could be easily fortified, the land was thoroughly isolated. Also, the river moved at a slow pace and was

54 THE CREATION OF CIVILIZATION

favored by an upstream breeze, making transportation by the river quite easy; the Nile was a highway as well as the center of an oasis. Such an area was easy to rule, and when the Egyptians come into historical view, we find them with a well-organized government.

Egyptian Government

The first historical figure we know of is the king, or pharaoh, *Menes* (MEE nees), who is reported to have unified the kingdoms of Upper and Lower Egypt. Menes founded the first Egyptian *dynasty,* a word meaning a group of rulers belonging to the same family. We know of him from his picture on a monumental plaque, or *stele* (STEE lee). The stele of Menes shows the pharaoh destroying his enemies single-handedly and commanding vast quantities of men and livestock. The pharaoh ruled without limitation; his government was that of an *absolute monarchy.*

Not only is the stele of Menes valuable as a source of information about the pharaoh, it is also an artistic reflection of the style and tone of Egyptian civilization. Both sides of the stele are shown here.

Marburg—Art Reference Bureau

The Egyptian concept of the pharaoh as god-king is evident in their sculpture and statuary. Representative of this concept is the pharaoh Chertihotep—strong, godlike and only remotely human.

The Role of the Pharaoh. The pharaoh, the cornerstone of Egyptian government and society, was not a servant of the gods but was considered to be a god himself. He was, the Egyptians believed, the son of *Re* (ray), the sun god, and upon his death, he joined the sun in its daily journey across the sky. The Egyptian government was a theocracy of the most thoroughgoing kind; the ruler was a god and the entire land his property. In addition to this divine status, the pharaoh had such an elaborate government under him that royal power endured even when the individual pharaoh was a weak person.

The reason for the power and stability of Egyptian government can be found in its bureaucracy as well as in its divinity. *Bureaucracy* is a word used to describe a collection of government officials who have strictly-prescribed tasks and who handle the routine matters of government. They are the people who collect taxes, pay the salaries of government officials, deliver mail and enforce laws. A bureaucracy is much like a machine following a fixed procedure and making no exceptions for individual cases. If a government is supported by a good bureaucracy, public affairs will continue to function on a day-to-day basis regardless of the capability of the actual ruler. A bureaucracy was a masterful human invention which enabled a ruler to govern a large number of people with whom he could have no direct personal contact.

The capital of Egypt during the Old Kingdom (2700-2200 B.C.) was Memphis, located near the mouth of the Nile. In this city, as in the cities of Sumer, many trades flourished. The fact that the interiors of Egyptian tombs have been found to contain non-Egyptian materials is proof that a successful trade, as well as many kinds of crafts, existed in ancient Egypt.

The Development of Writing. Running a large government produced the need for a class of scribes who could keep written records and teach others to write. Egyptian writing did not employ an alphabet but rather had pictures to stand for things and ideas. These symbols, or pictographs, originally stood for the actual item to be written. As time went on, certain pictures stood for syllables and could be used to make up different words. Egyptian writing was called *hieroglyphics;* it was written both on stone and on a product called *papyrus*. Papyrus, a word from which our word "paper" is derived, was made from a plant which grew near the river.

The following document containing some advice from a father to his son shows not only the power of literacy but also indicates the divisions in society which civilization can bring about. The simple equality of Neolithic life was forever gone, and just as the Sumerian schoolboy was urged on in his studies so that he could be superior to his brothers, the Egyptian father says to his son:

> I have never seen the smith as an ambassador, but I have seen the smith at his work at the mouth of his furnace, his fingers like the crocodiles, and he stank more than fish eggs. The stonemason finds his work in every kind of hard stone. When he has finished his labours, his arms are worn out . . . and he sleeps all doubled up until sunrise. . . . Therefore, apply your heart to learning. In truth there is nothing that can compare with it. If you have profited by a single day at school, it is a gain for eternity.

In spite of a high degree of specialization, with many people doing many different things, Egyptian society was not the kind of open and free society that ours is. Each man had his task—his place in the social structure—and since the government was ruled by a divine person, all activity was well regulated, and there could be no thought of any change. Artisans and laborers worked for the state, and even trade was controlled by the pharaoh. King Louis XIV of France is reported to have said, "I am the State." In many ways, he was not, but any pharaoh during the early period of Egyptian history could have made such a comment with complete truth. Farmers and craftsmen did not consciously offer their services to the government; rather they and their skills had no real existence outside the government; they were an integral part of the theocracy.

The Pyramids

This unity of Egyptian society can be best seen in the pyramids, those massive structures which dominate our knowledge of Egypt. Of the seven wonders of the ancient world, they are the only ones remaining. They have outlasted the civilization of the ancient Egyptians by centuries, and they could outlast the human race itself. The pyramids are a massive archaeological record, and from them, much can be learned about Egypt.

The pyramid was a tomb. The palaces of the pharaohs have vanished, but their tombs were built so well that they have remained. This fact alone should suggest something about Egyptian culture. The pharaoh *Cheops* (KEE ahps), who ruled in the 2600's B.C., had the power to walk into the desert, mark off an area 750 feet square, and rest assured that a pyramid consisting of two million blocks of limestone, each block weighing about two tons, would be ready to receive his body upon his death. Confronted by this colossal fact, we must ask, How could this be done? Why was it done? and What does it all signify?

Construction. During the time of the flooding of the Nile, no farming could take place, and so the manpower of the nation could be used to mine and cut the stones, float them down the river, drag them across the desert and put them into place. Simple enough—but consider for a moment all that is implied in this. First of all, the mathematical and engineering knowledge had to be developed to design the building and supervise its construction. The burst of intellectual power which produced the pyramids is without parallel in the history of the world. For hundreds of thousands of years, man had lived in wood buildings, if any. In the space of a few hundred years, building in stone was not only invented, but a structure was erected which was to remain the highest building in the world until very recent times.

Second, thousands of men had to be recruited, transported, fed, housed and kept at work for a period of over twenty years—the

Marburg—Art Reference Bureau

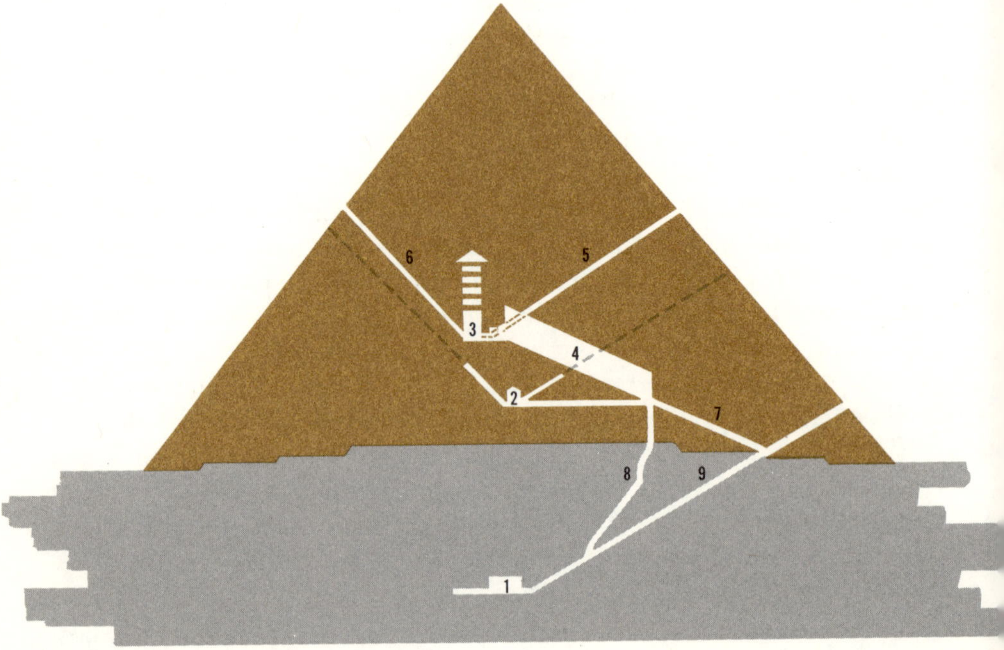

time needed to build such a massive structure. The two-ton blocks had to be moved into place and raised to a great height, all without the use of either the wheel or a system of pulleys. Under similar physical conditions, modern governments and social systems could probably not accomplish this feat. No better testament to the power of the Egyptian pharaoh or the efficiency of Egyptian bureaucracy can be found than a pyramid itself.

The Pyramids As Tombs. The fact that the pyramid was a tomb for the pharaoh tells us much about his role in Egyptian society. The body of the king had to have a resting place which would last forever, completely conquering the ravages of time. Since the pyramids are still here, the Egyptians succeeded in this quest. The place where the king spent his earthly life was unimportant compared with the place where he would spend eternity. Inside the burial vault itself, hidden deep within the pyramid, all the implements which the king had used were placed with his body; the walls were adorned with scenes of his earthly life, and he was provided with a large boat in which to make his daily course through the sky once he had joined his father, the sun god. The soul of the king, the *ka* (kah) as the Egyptians called it, would leave the tomb but would return to the body from time to time. Therefore, the body was preserved by a process of embalming called *mummification*. Preservatives and the dry climate of Egypt have both worked to give the pharaohs a kind of immortality. The mummies today displayed in museums have served their purpose well; they have conquered the power of time.

The Significance of the Pyramids. The pyramid, therefore, is a powerful illustration of the Egyptian belief in the existence of life after death. The pharaoh was not really a human being, and alive or dead, he was the ruler of Egypt. As the Egyptians said, he was "the god by whom one lives," the god whose perpetual well-being determined the well-being of the nation. Did then the

---

Remnants of an earlier age, the pyramids shown at the top of page 58 dwarf the fields around them. The diagram below the photo shows the interior of the pyramid of Cheops. Included were two incomplete burial chambers (1 and 2) and a final burial chamber (3). The Grand Gallery (4) led to the final burial chamber, which was ventilated by two narrow air shafts (5 and 6). After the pharaoh's body was interred, workmen sealed up the Ascending Corridor (7) with stone plugs weighing several tons, then descended through a shaft (8) and to the outside through the Descending Corridor (9).

Egyptians work willingly in building these tombs? This is a difficult question to answer because the average Egyptian never wrote down his thoughts for us to examine. Just because we would not work on a tomb for a political leader as an Egyptian would, we should not think that the pyramids were built by forced labor. We have no evidence of any attempt among the people to revolt or to resist the demands of the god-king. People today in our own society will permit one-fifth or more of their wealth to go to the government to provide for their safety and well-being. Individuals have generally been willing to serve in the armed forces and give their lives for the sake of their country. Is this sacrifice any less than the labor of the Egyptian on the pyramid? The very existence of the theocratic Egyptian state depended upon the actions of the pharaoh as a mortal king and as an immortal god.

The pyramid not only illustrates the power of the government, the organization of society and the strength of religious beliefs, but it is in itself evidence of the security and isolation of Egypt. If it had been necessary to use men for frequent wars, the labor required to build such a structure would not have been available. Egyptian culture was permitted to work out its own forms for centuries without interference from others and with little contact with the outside world. During the long period of early Egyptian history (3000-2200 B.C.), the isolation of Egypt from other civilizations fostered the development of distinctive and strong forms of art, religion, government and thought which could not be easily changed in later times. Much of the culture of Egypt remained the same or almost unchanged throughout its entire history.

To the Egyptian, his country was the center of the universe and the most blessed of places. To the west was Libya, inhabited by nomads. To the south, above the first cataract along the Nile, was Nubia, inhabited by tribes who served only as a slave supply.

The degree of Egyptian isolation can be seen in their language. The word for south is the same as "up-stream." When the Egyptian heard of lands with rivers running to the south (instead of to the north as the Nile did), he regarded these as backward lands. There was no such thing as rain in the Egyptian vocabulary; other lands merely had a "Nile in the sky." This kind of pride in one's own way of life may appear to be arrogant, but in judging other people by their own standards, the Egyptians were not unlike us. When speaking of people in other lands, do we not say that they do things differently from us, and not that we do things differently from them?

Even though the pyramids are the most striking accomplishments of the Egyptians, these people did more than develop a social and political organization which could build pyramids. They constructed a religious system, including a pantheon of gods and a mythology; they also developed an impressive literature.

Religious Beliefs

The creator god in Egyptian thought was *Atum* (AH tuhm), who first appeared on a small hillock as it emerged from the watery deep. From this small island, Atum created the other gods. No doubt this account of creation was developed from a sight the Egyptians saw each year when the receding waters of the Nile would cause small hillocks of land to appear as the fertility of the soil was recreated.

The Importance of Re. The sun god Re, we have seen, was a most important god who moved across the sky each day and passed through the waters under the earth each night. According to the Egyptians, the flat earth was held up by a body of water from which the Nile gushed forth at its source. Each evening after the sun god had reached the west, he moved beneath the earth and then had to struggle with an evil serpent who tried to destroy him. The outcome of this battle was not known until the next morning when Re emerged victorious. This dramatic action of Re and his obvious life-giving powers made him an important god in the Egyptian pantheon. The pharaoh was the son of Re, and after his death, he was equipped with the boat to perform his important daily function. The following hymn celebrates the triumph of Re.

> Thou risest, thou risest brilliant over thy enemies.
> Thou causes the day boat to sail past,
> And repellest the dragon at the storm of nighttime;
> He cannot approach at the decisive moment;
> Thou hast destroyed the power of the enemies;
> The antagonists of Re are overthrown by the
>   flame of terror.

There were thousands of lesser gods in the Egyptian religion, ranging from small animals to the Nile itself. Many of these were local deities having no power beyond a small area, and many were used for purposes of magic and superstition, the universal religion of the ignorant. The sheer number of Egyptian gods is beyond our comprehension, for the Egyptians accepted *polytheism* (a belief in many gods) as unthinkingly as many people today accept *monotheism* (a belief in one God). The Egyptians never got rid of old forms when new ideas were added. Many of the gods were represented in the form of animals, and this may have been a carry-over from the totemism of a past age. Isolated from the bracing effect of the infusion of new ideas, the Egyptians continued along their own way, adding to their culture, but changing very little.

Scarcely any mythology grew up around the Egyptian gods, and with few exceptions, the gods do not have dramatic stories told about them; they remain as names rather than as distinct personalities. Egyptian literary energy seemed to be directed to stories in which the gods were not involved. Nonetheless, some Egyptian myths did concern the gods. The following is an example of a myth describing the creation of the moon.

> Then his majesty the (sun) god said: "Pray summon Thoth." He was brought immediately. Then his majesty the god said to Thoth: "Behold, I am in the sky in my place. As I am going to take the light to the Underworld . . . thou shalt be in my place as a substitute, and thou shalt be called the substitute of Re. . . . Moreover, I will make thee to extend thy power over the primordial gods, though they are greater than thou. . . . I will make thee to encompass the heavens with thy beauty and thy rays. Thou shalt be my substitute, the faces of all who look upon thee shall see by thee, so that the eye of every man shall praise god through thee."

The Isis-Osiris Myth. Being an agricultural people, the Egyptians were concerned with the annual death and rebirth of nature. The most popular of Egyptian gods associated with the cycle of nature were *Isis* (I suhs) and *Osiris* (oh SI ruhs), and the following story forms the basis of an important myth.

> Osiris was a king who was hated by his brother, Seth. One day during a feast, Seth produced a beautiful coffin and offered to give it to the person who could fit it perfectly. Many men tried the coffin, but when Osiris got in, Seth quickly closed the door, locking him inside. He vanished with the captured king, and Isis, the loving wife of Osiris, searched throughout the land trying to find her husband. When she found him, he was dead. Isis hovered over her husband and through the strength of her love restored him to life, but not enough for him to resume his rule in the world. Osiris then descended to the underworld and became the judge and ruler of the dead. Horus, the son of Osiris and Isis, avenged his father's death and killed Seth. Horus then became the ruler of the world while Osiris presided over the final judgment in the land of the dead.

The story itself is a moving tale of devotion which had a wide appeal throughout Egyptian history. Even after the end of Egyptian history proper, the worship of Isis was a significant cult in the Roman Empire. The existence of Horus, the son, in the tale is an early example of a holy family, a concept which was also found in later cultures.

The main theme of the myth is that of death and rebirth. The separation of Isis and Osiris occurs during the season when no crops could grow, when the soil was not fertile. The return of Osiris to life was associated with the rebirth of the soil's fertility. It was no accident that temples of Osiris were usually built close to the Nile. In addition to being a nature myth, the story concerned human life in that Osiris became the judge of the dead. Egyptians hoped to imitate Osiris and so to gain eternal life, just as nature itself never remained dead but was always reborn. This theme of death and resurrection, once associated with nature, was also a powerful and long-lasting motif in the history of religions.

Life After Death. Every Egyptian hoped for a life after death, and his religious system gave some substance to this hope. The tombs of Egyptians were not only decorated with scenes from earthly life, but the coffins were filled with religious texts containing the proper words necessary to speed the ka through its journey to the land of eternal life. Once the soul of a man had reached the judgment, his heart (which, according to the Egyptian mind, could be in two places at the same time) was weighed on a balance against a feather. If the heart was lighter than the feather, the soul would gain eternal life; if it was heavier, some kind of punishment was inflicted. The importance of eternity in Egyptian thought can be seen in the following advice given to an Egyptian king.

> Put not your faith in length of years, for the gods regard a lifetime as but an hour. A man surviveth after reaching the haven of death, and for sole treasure there are laid beside him his deeds. Eternal is the existence yonder, and he who has made light of it is a fool. But as for him who has reached it without wrongdoing, he shall continue yonder like a god, stepping forward boldly like the lords of eternity.

The Egyptians believed that in many cases, eternal life was gained by the knowledge and correct performance of the proper rituals and formulas, copies of which were buried with the body to act as passports to eternity. However, the belief grew that a good life was necessary for a person to gain eternal life; this belief can be seen in the following famous prayer, called the *Negative Confession.*

> Hail to thee O Great God, lord of the Two Justices!
> I have come to thee my lord, I have been brought that
> I might see thy beauty. I know thee; I know thy name
> and the names of the forty-two gods who are with thee
> in the Broad Hall of the Two Justices who live on
> them who preserve evil, and who drink their blood on
> that day of reckoning up character in the presence of
> Osiris.... I have brought thee justice. I have
> expelled deceit for thee.
>
> I have not committed evil against men.
> I have not mistreated cattle.
> I have not committed sin in the place of truth.
> I have not made anyone sick.
> I have not made anyone weep.
> I have not cut down the food income in the temples.
> I have not shared the birds of the gods.
> I have not built a dam against running water.
> I have not held up water in its season.
> I have given no order to a killer.
> I have not taken the loaves of the blessed dead.
> I have not taken milk from the mouths of children.
>
> . . . .
>
> Evil will never happen to me in this land or in this
> Broad Hall of the Two Justices, because I know the names
> of these Gods who are in it, the followers of the Great
> God.
>
> O Wide-of-Stride, who comes forth from Heliopolis,
>   I have not committed evil.
> O Eater-of-Blood, who comes forth from the execution block,
>   I have not slain the cattle of the god.
> O Wanderer, who comes forth from Bubastis,
>   I have not gossiped.
> O Mischief-Maker, who comes forth from the sanctuary,
>   I have not been overheated.
> O High of Head serpent, who comes forth from the cavern,
>   My portion has not been too large, not even
>   in my own property.
>
> . . . .
>
> "Come," says Thoth, "why hast thou come?"
> "I have come here to be announced."
> "What is thy condition?"
> "I am pure of sin. I have protected myself from the
>   strife of those who are in their days. I am not
>   among them."

"Then to whom shall I announce thee? I shall announce
thee to (him whose) ceiling is of fire, (whose)
walls are living serpents, and whose pavement is
water."
"Who is he?"
"He is Osiris. Then go thou, Behold, thou are announced."

From this confession, we can conclude that the Egyptians believed that a proper life would gain eternity for the soul. However, the recitation of good actions, or at least the lack of bad actions, could become merely an empty ritual performed by anyone, good or bad. To many Egyptians, just memorizing the forty-two gods might have been the most important action with which to gain eternal life and to pass with safety through the Hall of the Two Justices. Yet, the *Negative Confession* shows that morality and ethics were important to the Egyptians and served some role in their religion.

Although much of Egyptian life, especially the absolute government and polytheistic religion, would probably repel us, the faces

This papyrus shows the weighing of the heart of a dead man. If the heart proved to be heavier than the feather (which symbolized truth), it would be devoured by the fierce creature on the right.

Art Reference Bureau, British Museum

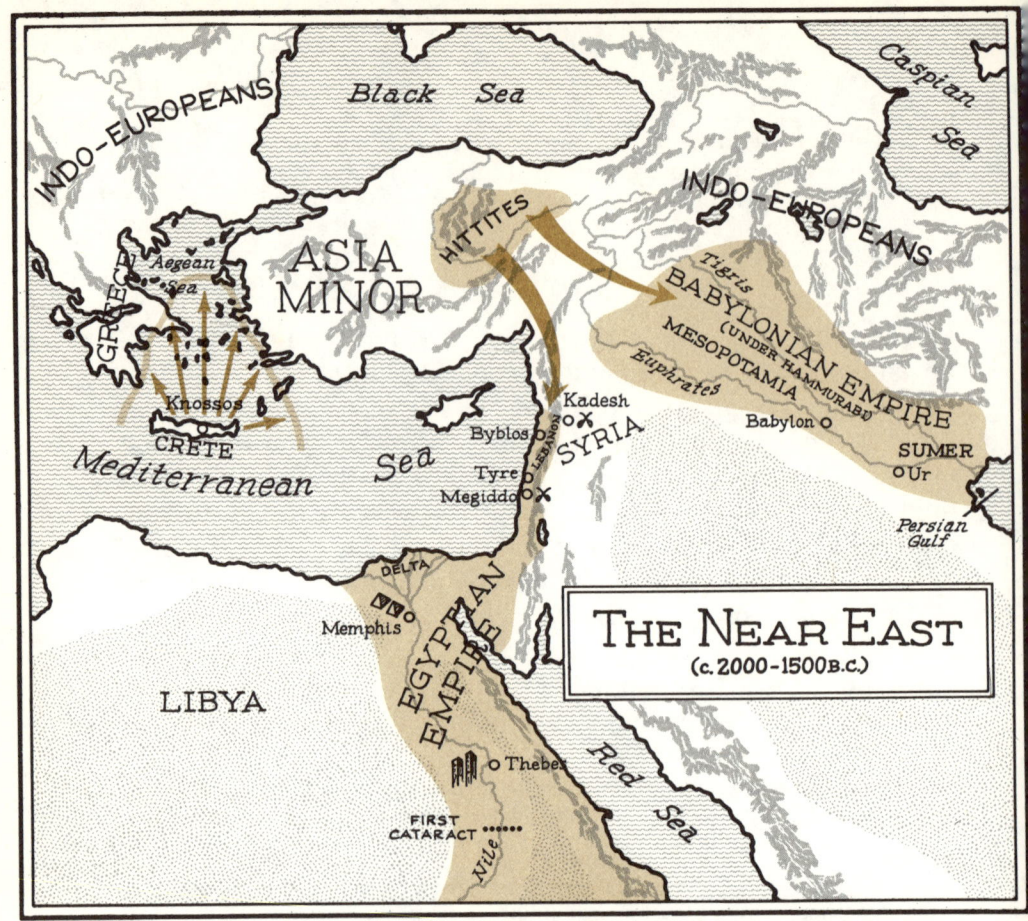

Between 2000 and 1500 B.C., the Hittites began to expand, invading and conquering Babylonia. Egypt's expanding empire defeated Syria at Megiddo but was halted by the Hittites at Kadesh many years later.

which look out at us from the pyramid paintings seem to indicate that these people enjoyed life and indulged in many pleasures which we would appreciate. As one Egyptian poet sang:

> Make holiday, verily, verily!
> Put incense and fine oil together beside thee
> And garlands of lotus and . . . flowers upon thy breast.
> The woman whom thou lovest,
> It is she who sits at thy side.
> Thou shouldst not anger thy heart
> Over anything that has happened.
> Put music before thee,
> Do not recall evil, abomination of the god;
> Bethink thee of joys,
> Thou righteous, thou just and true man,

> Calm, friendly, content, relaxed,
> Happy, not speaking evil.
> Give drunkenness to thy heart every day
> Until the day comes in which there is landing!

Perhaps it is the fact that the Egyptians could regard death as a "landing" which made them enjoy their life so very much. At least this was one poet's opinion.

Religion, although it was very important to the Egyptians, did not command all of their creative energies. Many of their wise sayings and proverbs point the way to good action on the basis of common sense rather than as commands from the gods. Consider, for example, the very human wisdom contained in this proverb.

> If thou art one to whom a petition is made, be calm as thou listenest to the petitioner's speech. Do not rebuff him before he has swept out his body or before he has said that for which he came. A petitioner likes attention to his words better than the fulfilling of that for which he came. . . . It is not (necessary) that everything about which he has petitioned should come to pass, (but) a good hearing is a soothing of the heart.

It is interesting to note that the most coherent piece of early Egyptian literature which has survived is a short story in which the gods are hardly mentioned—"The Story of Sinuhe." Perhaps the most charming creation of the Egyptians, in fact, was the short story, a literary form which they apparently invented.

In conclusion, we see that the third millennium B.C. was perhaps the most creative period in the whole of human history. Two cultures, Sumerian and Egyptian, broke out of forms which had existed for hundreds of thousands of years and, in so doing, became civilized. The two civilizations which developed had much in common, although they also show the different shapes which civilization can take. Both the Sumerians and the Egyptians have had a great influence on the shape of later civilization, including our own.

Define

Menes
dynasty
absolute monarchy
Re
bureaucracy

hieroglyphics
Cheops
polytheism
monotheism
Osiris

Review and Answer

1. What is the difference between a monarchy and a bureaucracy?
2. In what ways has the River Nile influenced Egyptian culture?
3. Apply the three questions suggested in the final paragraph of Chapter Three (What is it? Why is it? What of it?) to the pyramids.
4. Explain the main theme of the Isis-Osiris myth.
5. Why is the *Negative Confession* an important document in the development of human culture?

Reading II

The telling of tales has always been a part of man's culture. Stories, passed on by word of mouth, served to keep alive the deeds of great men, to pass on ideas or values, or to provide pleasure. The Egyptians were the first people to use the literary form we call the short story. "The Story of Sinuhe" tells of a man who left Egypt because he was fearful that the new pharaoh would not be favorable to him. Sinuhe lived in a foreign land, had many adventures, but eventually returned to Egypt when he became old. This story tells us about many values held by the Egyptians, and it breathes the atmosphere of that ancient land. The theme of the story, travel and homecoming, even today serves as the basis for works of literature.

The story was translated from a hieroglyphic manuscript, the major portions of which are in the Berlin Museum. The style of writing is often stiff, and the choice of words at times seems awkward. However, we must remember that the story speaks to us from a great distance and had to be translated from a language which was very different from our own. It is one of man's earliest written stories.

"The Story of Sinuhe"

Year 30, Third Month of the First Season, Day 7. The god ascended to his horizon, the King of Upper and Lower Egypt: Sehetepib-Re was taken up to heaven and united with the sun disc. The body of the god merged with him who made him. The Residence City was in silence, hearts were in mourning, the Great Double Doors were sealed shut. The courtiers sat head upon lap, and the people were in grief.

Now his majesty had sent an army to the land of the Temeh-Libyans, with his eldest son as the commander thereof, the good god Sen-Usert, and even now he was returning and had carried off living captives of the Tehenu-Libyans and all kinds of cattle without number.

The courtiers of the palace were sent to the western border to let the King's Son know the events which had taken place at the court. The messengers met him on the road, and they reached him in the evening time. He did not delay a moment; the falcon flew away with his attendants, without letting his army know it. Now the royal children who had been following him in this army had been sent for, and one of them was summoned. While I was standing nearby I heard his voice as he was speaking and I was a little way off. My heart was distraught, my arms spread out in dismay, trembling fell upon all my limbs. I removed myself by leaps and bounds to seek a hiding place for myself. I placed myself between two bushes, in order to cut myself off from the road and its travel.

John A. Wilson, trans., in J. B. Pritchard, ed., *Ancient Near Eastern Texts Relating to the Old Testament* (Princeton: Princeton University Press, 1955), pp. 19-22. Reprinted by permission of Princeton University Press.

I set out southward, but I did not plan to reach this Residence City, for I thought that there would be civil disorder, and I did not expect to live after him. I crossed Lake Ma'aty near Sycamore, and I came to Snefru Island. I spent the day there on the edge of the fields. I came into open light, while it was still day, and I met a man standing near by. He stood in awe of me, for he was afraid. When the time of the evening meal came, I drew near to OX-town. I crossed over in a barge without a rudder, by aid of the west wind. I passed by the east of the quarry above Mistress-of-the-Red-Mountain. I gave free road to my feet going northward, and I came up to the Wall-of-the Ruler, made to oppose the Asiatics and to crush the Sand-Crossers. I took a crouching position in a bush, for fear lest the watchmen upon the wall where their day's duty was might see me.

I set out at evening time, and when day broke I reached Peten. I halted at the Island of Kem-wer. An attack of thirst overtook me. I was parched, and my throat was dusty. I said: "This is the taste of death!" But then I lifted up my heart and collected myself, for I had heard the sound of the lowing of cattle, and I spied Asiatics. The sheikh among them, who had been in Egypt, recognized me. Then he gave me water while he boiled milk for me. I went with him to his tribe. What they did for me was good.

One foreign country gave me to another. I set off for Byblos and approached Qedem, and spent a year and a half there. Ammi-enshi—he was a ruler of Upper Retenu—took me and said to me: "Thou wilt do well with me and thou wilt hear the speech of Egypt." He said this for he knew my character, he had heard of my wisdom, and the people of Egypt who were there with him had borne witness for me. . . .

He set me at the head of his children. He married me to his eldest daughter. He let me choose for myself of his country, of the choicest of that which was with him on his frontier with another country. It was a good land, named Yaa. Figs were in it, and grapes. It had more wine than water. Plentiful was its honey, abundant its olives. Every kind of fruit was on its trees. Barley was there and emmer. There was no limit to any kind of cattle. Moreover, great was that which accrued to me as a result of the love of me. He made me ruler of a tribe of the choicest of his country. Bread was made for me as daily fare, wine as daily provision, cooked meat and roast fowl, beside the wild beasts of the desert, for they hunted for me and laid before me, beside the catch of my own hounds. Many . . . were made for me, and milk in every kind of cooking. I spent many years, and my children grew up to be strong men, each as the restrainer of his own tribe. The messenger who went north or who went south to the Residence City stopped over with me, for I used to make everybody stop over. I gave water to the thirsty. I put him who had strayed back on the road. I rescued him who had been robbed. When the Asiatics became so bold as to oppose the rulers of foreign countries, I counseled their movements. This ruler of Retenu had me spend many years as commander of his army. Every foreign country against which I went forth, when I had made my attack on it, was driven away from its pasturage and its well. I plundered its cattle, carried off its inhabitants, took away their food, and slew people in it by my strong arm, by my bow, by my movements, and by my successful plans. I found favor in his heart, he loved me, he recognized my valor, and he placed me at the head of his children, when he saw how my arms flourished.

A mightly man of Retenu came, that he might challenge me in my own camp. He was a hero without his peer, and he had repelled all of it. He said that he would fight me, he intended to despoil me, and he planned to plunder my cattle, on the advice of his tribe. That prince discussed it with me, and I said: "I do not know him. Certainly I am no confederate of his, so that I might move freely in his encampment. Is it the case that I have ever opened his door or overthrown his fences? Rather, it is hostility because he sees me carrying out thy commissions. I am really like a stray bull in the midst of another herd, and a bull of these cattle attacks him...."

During the night I strung my bow and shot my arrows. I gave free play to my dagger, and polished my weapons. When day broke, Retenu was come. It had whipped up its tribes and collected the countries of a good half of it. It had thought only of this fight. Then he came to me as I was waiting, for I had placed myself near him. Every heart burned for me; women and men groaned. Every heart was sick for me. They said: "Is there another strong man who could fight against him?" Then he took his shield, his battle-axe, and his armful of javelins. Now after I had let his weapons issue forth, I made his arrows pass by me uselessly, one close to another. He charged me, and I shot him, my arrow sticking in his neck. He cried out and fell on his nose. I felled him with his own battle-axe and raised my cry of victory over his back, while every Asiatic roared. I gave praise to Montu while his adherents were mourning for him. This ruler, Ammi-enshi, took me into his embrace. Then I carried off his goods and plundered his cattle. What he had planned to do to me I did to him. I took what was in his tent and stripped his encampment. I became great thereby, I became extensive in my wealth, I became abundant in my cattle....

Now when the majesty of the King of Upper and Lower Egypt ... was told about his situation in which I was, then his majesty kept sending to me with presentations from the royal presence, that he might gladden the heart of this servant like the ruler of any foreign country— "Do you return to Egypt, that thou mayest see the home in which thou didst grow up, and kiss the ground at the Great Double Door and join with the courtiers. For today surely, thou hast begun to grow old; thou hast lost thy virility. Recall thou the day of burial, the passing to a revered state, when the evening is set aside for thee with ointments and wrapping from the hands of Tait. A funeral procession is made for thee on the day of burial, a mummy case of gold, with head of lapis-lazuli, with a heaven above thee, as thou art placed upon a sledge, oxen dragging thee and singers in front of thee.... When the requirements of the offering table are summoned for thee, and there is sacrifice beside thy offering stones, thy pillars being hewn of white stone in the midst of the tombs of the royal children. It should not be that thou shouldest die in a foreign country. Asiatics should not escort thee. Thou shouldest not be placed in a sheepskin when thy wall is made. This is too long to be roaming the earth. Give head to sickness, that thou mayest return."

This decree reached me as I was standing in the midst of my tribe. It was read to me. I put myself upon my belly; I touched the ground; I scattered it upon my hair. "How can this be done for a servant whom his heart led astray to barbarous countries?"

Then they came for this servant. . . . I was permitted to spend a day in Yaa handing over my property to my children, my eldest son being responsible for my tribe. My tribe and all my property were in his charge; my serfs, all my cattle, my fruit, and every pleasant tree of mine.

Then this servant came southward. I halted at the "Ways of Horus." The commander there who was responsible for the patrol sent a message to the Residence to make it known. Then his majesty sent a capable overseer of peasants of the palace, with loaded ships in his train, carrying presentations from the royal presence for the Asiatics who had followed me, escorting me to the "Ways of Horus." I called each of them by his name. Every butler was busy at his duties. When I started and set sail, the kneading and straining of beer was carried on beside me, until I had reached the town of Lisht.

When day had broken, very early, they came and summoned me to the palace. I put my brow to the ground between the sphinxes, while the royal children were waiting in a recess to meet me. The courtiers who usher into the audience hall set me on the way to the private chambers. I found his majesty upon the Great Throne in a recess of fine gold. When I was stretched out upon my belly, I knew not myself in his presence, although this god greeted me pleasantly. I was like a man caught in the dark; my soul departed, my body was powerless, my heart was not in my body, that I might know life from death.

Then his majesty said to one of these courtiers: "Lift him up. Let him speak to me." Then his majesty said: "Behold, thou art come. Thou has trodden the foreign countries and made a fight. But now elderliness has attacked thee; thou hast reached old age. It is no small matter that thy corpse be properly buried; thou shouldst not be interred by bowmen. Do not, do not act thus any longer: for thou dost not speak when thy name is pronounced!" Yet I was afraid to respond, and I answered it with the answer of one afraid: "What is it that my lord says to me? I should answer it, but there is nothing that I can do: it is really the hand of a god. It is terror that is in my belly like that which produced the fated flight. Behold, I am before thee. Thine is life. May thy majesty do as he pleases."

Thereupon the royal children were ushered in. Then his majesty said to the Queen: "Here is Si-nuhe, come as a Bedu, in the guise of the Asiatics." She gave a very great cry, and the royal children clamored all together. Then they said to his majesty: "It is not really he, O Sovereign, my lord!" Then his majesty said: "It is really he!" Now when they had brought with them their bead-necklaces, their rattles, and their sistra, then they presented them to his majesty. . . . Then his majesty said:

"He shall not fear. He has no title to be in dread. He shall be a courtier among the nobles. He shall be put in the ranks of the courtiers."

So I went forth from the midst of the inner chambers, with the young children giving me their hands. Thereafter we went to the Great Double Door. I was put into the house of a royal son, in which were splendid things. A cool room was in it, and images of the horizon. Costly things of the Treasury were in it. Clothing of royal linen, myrrh, and prime oil of the king and of the nobles whom he loves were in every room. Every butler was busy at his duties. Years were made to pass away from my body. I was plucked, and my hair was combed. A load of dirt was given to the desert, and my clothes to the Sand-Crossers. I was clad in fine linen and annointed with prime oil. I slept in a bed. I gave up the sand to them who are in it, and wood oil to him who is anointed with it. I was given a house which had a garden, which had been in the possession of a courtier. Many craftsmen built it, and all its woodwork was newly restored. Meals were brought to me from the palace three or four times a day, apart from that which the royal children gave, without ceasing a moment.

There was constructed for me a pyramid-tomb of stone in the midst of the pyramid-tombs. The stone masons who hew a pyramid-tomb took over its ground area. The outline-draftsmen designed in it; the chief sculptors carved in it; and the overseers of works who are in the necropolis made it their concern. Its necessary materials were made from all the outfittings which are placed at a tomb-shaft. Mortuary priests were given to me. There was made for me a necropolis garden, with fields in it formerly extending as far as the town, like that which is done for a chief courtier. My statue was overlaid with gold, and its skirt was of fine gold. It was his majesty who had it made. There is no poor man for whom the like has been done.

So I was under the favor of the king's presence until the day of mooring had come.

The original "Story of Sinuhe" was written in hieroglyphics on a tablet such as the one shown here.

Courtesy, Museum of Fine Arts, Boston, Sears Fund

In the unit just finished, we have seen the birth of two civilizations and have sketched out their main characteristics as they evolved during the third millennium B.C. In this unit, we will move into the second millennium and see how man added to, or elaborated, the civilization which he inherited. In this account, we will have an opportunity to probe more deeply into the nature of civilization and to have a more intensive look at the record of human history.

Not all people or groups of people can be discussed in this account, as history is a process of selection; all the facts can never be recorded in any one book. Up to a point, a student must trust the book he is reading in the hope that a good selection of facts has been made. He must then go beyond the textbook and seek out information for himself. He must make his own history.

UNIT III
The Elaboration of Civilization

6

Babylonia and Beyond

The need for certain kinds of materials led the Sumerians to send merchants into the less civilized areas around them. The surrounding barbarian peoples supplied the Sumerians with raw materials in return for food or for the finished products which only a civilized people could make. This kind of economic contact led the pastoral and mountain-dwelling barbarians to envy the wealth and luxury which the river-based people in Mesopotamia had gained. Goods and knowledge were exchanged by means of trade, the arts of civilization moved out from the river valleys and new peoples moved into the civilized areas. At times, this process was accomplished by war.

The Babylonian Empire

The pastoral people living around Mesopotamia belonged to a large group of people called *Semites,* so called because of the basic similarity of their languages, which belong to the Semitic linguistic group. The civilized Sumerian had a low opinion of his neighbors, yet about the year 2500 B.C., Semitic people began to invade the land of Sumer, thereby substituting war for trade as a means of communication. In time, the Sumerians vanished, and the Semitic element in Mesopotamian culture became predominant. However, most of the higher elements of culture, such as art, religion and mythology, followed Sumerian forms, and the Sumerian language itself remained alive for some time as a second language used by learned scribes.

Government. The conquerors of Sumer were aggressive people who organized their society into large states. Kings took the place of priests as rulers and attempted to extend their rule beyond Mesopotamia. Around the year 1800 B.C., the city of Babylon, once a small town on the fringe of the Sumerian civilization, became the capital of a large empire. The most famous Babylonian king was Hammurabi, whose royal government commanded a large staff of officials and soldiers. The Babylonian kings were no longer ruling small city-states but commanded instead large empires; from this time on, absolute monarchy became the standard form of government in Mesopotamia.

Babylonian merchants moved far from home, and the presence of these traders as far away as Asia Minor increased the needs of government. If traders were attacked or captured, or if barbarians refused to supply materials, demands were put upon the government at home to act, either to protect the merchants or to secure needed materials. In this way, the stretching of economic needs led to a demand for a greater spread of government. As more backward people were introduced to the pleasures of civilization, there was a greater threat of invasion and war. Therefore, as the second millennium B.C. progressed, civilization was demanding from man more cultural inventions in order to manage it.

In spite of the power of the Babylonian kings, Mesopotamian government never developed the strength and security that the Egyptian government enjoyed. In Mesopotamia, the king was not a god, and the land was not isolated by geographic barriers. Although the Mesopotamian social structure was far more fixed than ours is today, it did not have the timeless rigidity which marked Egyptian society. Different peoples moved in and out of the area, merchants were not completely controlled by the government and even the king himself could be toppled from power.

The Code of Hammurabi. To cope with the growth of Babylonian society, Hammurabi had all the laws of the land gathered

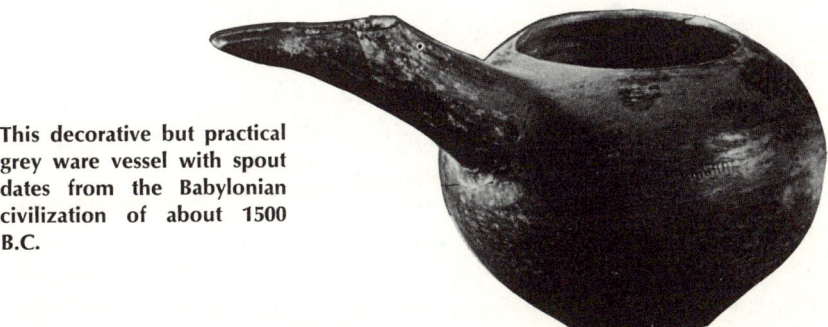

This decorative but practical grey ware vessel with spout dates from the Babylonian civilization of about 1500 B.C.

The University Museum, Philadelphia

together, simplified and written down so that they were clear and unalterable. Such a process is called *codification*. *Hammurabi's Code*, a collection of laws which the Babylonians believed were given to him on a mountaintop by the gods, is the first example in history of a complete recording of laws. In a small community, written laws are not necessary because the customs of the land are usually understood and agreed upon by all. However, when a society becomes large and complex, laws which are not written down can be twisted by judges, usually to favor the rich and powerful. Hammurabi's Code, engraved on a stele and supposedly having authority from the gods, could not be altered; justice could then be given to all. The code was designed to cover all situations. In spite of the fact that the code vanished when the Babylonian empire was destroyed, this concept of unchangeable laws, in written form, was a major achievement in the development of civilization.

Hammurabi's Code provides a mirror of Babylonian society, just as the wall paintings in Egyptian tombs were a reflection of Egyptian life. An imaginative reading of some of these laws should enable us to see how another society governed itself. Two of the laws are quoted here. What conclusions about Babylonian society can be drawn from them?

> If a builder constructed a house for a man, but did not make his work strong, with the result that the house which he built collapsed and so has caused the death of the owner of the house, that builder shall be put to death.
> If it has caused the death of a son of the owner of the house they shall put the son of that builder to death.

The code itself is prefaced by a majestic prologue. Some of the gods mentioned in the prologue, such as Anu and Enlil, are Sumerian; others, however, for example *Marduk* (MAR dook) and *Shamash*, have Semitic names. Thus, we can see how the Babylonians added to the previous creations of the Sumerians. The gods of the sun, moon and planet Venus were important celestial deities. The Babylonians gave them the Semitic names of Shamash, Sin (seen) and Ishtar, respectively. To the Babylonians, a planet was not "it," but rather "she." The planet Venus was the goddess Ishtar, who disappeared from the heavens during the season when no crops would grow. The Babylonians believed that she descended into the underworld during this season and returned only when the crops grew and the harvest came. Ishtar was an important nature goddess.

As the city of Babylon grew in importance and finally became the center of an empire, the city-god, Marduk, became the major god in the Babylonian pantheon. His strength was directly related to the military and political power of Babylon. When the empire declined, the worship of Marduk declined with it. In the ancient world, the power of gods usually rose and fell with the success of their worshippers.

Mythology. The fullest and most impressive Babylonian myth, one which is perhaps the most significant and exciting of all early myths, is the creation story. An account of creation is called a *cosmogony* (not to be confused with cosomolgy) in that it tells of the *origin* of the universe. According to Babylonian cosmogony, Marduk created the universe out of a watery chaos. In the myth, the watery chaos was represented by the goddess Tiamat (TYAH maht). Marduk's destruction of Tiamat was, no doubt, a mythical version of the struggle with the waters of the Euphrates which had been undertaken by the original settlers of Mesopotamia.

What we have seen of Babylonian literature so far has dealt mainly with the gods: man is barely mentioned in the creation myth. If this were all we knew about these people, we might conclude that they saw man as an insignificant creature existing only to serve the gods. But we know more of the Babylonians than this. Archaeologists have found tablets telling the story of a warrior king, a human being named *Gilgamesh*. This man built cities, slew a monster and even challenged the gods in his quest for knowledge and immortality.

A long narrative poem about men who perform heroic deeds and who grapple with the fate marked out for them by destiny or by the gods is called an *epic*. An epic usually tells of a hero who lived in the past and whose way of life reflects the values held by a civilization. Most peoples have stories of heroes who lived in the past and who continue to live in the minds of men through the retelling of epic poems. For the Greeks, it was the heroes of the *Iliad* and *Odyssey;* for Europeans, it was, and still is, the tales of Beowulf, of Roland and of King Arthur. In ancient Babylonia, the Sumerian legend of Gilgamesh was expanded into a full epic poem, the first example of this type of literature.

The Epic of Gilgamesh. Gilgamesh is described in the epic as a man so mighty that no one could withstand his wishes. The people cried out to the gods to create another person who would be as strong. In response, the gods created the man Enkidu (EN key doo), an uncivilized person who lived in the woods. In order to bring him out of his savage state, a woman was sent to lure him away. The civilizing of Enkidu might well have been the Babylonian portrayal of the coming of mankind into a civilized state.

After Enkidu had spent some time with a civilized human being, he tried to return to nature—without much success.

> Then, when the gazelles saw him, they bolted away; when the wild creatures saw him, they fled. Enkidu would have followed, but his body was bound as though with a cord, his knees gave way when he started to run, his swiftness was gone. And now the wild creatures had all fled away; Enkidu was grown weak, for wisdom was with him, and the thoughts of a man were in his heart.
> And now the woman said to Enkidu, "When I look at you you have become like a god. Why do you yearn to run wild again with the beast in the hills? Get up from the ground, the bed of a shepherd." He listened to her words with care. It was good advice that she gave. She divided her clothing in two and with the one half she clothed him and with the other herself; and holding his hand she led him like a mother to the sheepfolds, and to the feeding place of the shepherds. There all the shepherds crowded round to see him, they put down bread in front of him, but Enkidu . . . fumbled and gaped, at a loss what to do or how he should eat the bread and drink the strong wine. Then the woman said, "Enkidu, eat bread; it is the staff of life; drink the wine; it is the custom of the land." So he ate till he was full and drank strong wine, seven goblets. He became merry, his heart exulted and his face shone. He rubbed down the matted hair of his body and anointed himself with oil. Enkidu had become a man.

Once Enkidu had been separated from nature, he had a longing for human companionship and was led to meet Gilgamesh. The two became friends and performed many heroic feats together. On one occasion, they even went deep into a forest and cut down some trees belonging to the sacred grove of a god. So powerful was Gilgamesh and his friend that the goddess Ishtar offered to marry Gilgamesh and make him immortal, but the hero refused, so much did he enjoy life and the companionship of his friend.

Enkidu eventually, as a human being, entertained a fear of death and then cursed the woman who had made him civilized and had taken him from his paradise, his Garden of Eden. One night, he had a dream, a vision of life after death.

> Last night I dreamed again, my friend. The heavens moaned and the earth replied; I stood alone before an awful being; his face was somber like the black bird of the storm. He fell upon me with the talons of an eagle and he held me fast, pinioned with his

claw, till I smothered; then he transformed me so that my arms became wings covered with feathers. He turned his stare towards me, and he led me away to the palace of Irkalla, the Queen of Darkness, to the house from which none who enters ever returns, down the road from which there is no coming back.

There is the house whose people sit in darkness; dust is their food and clay their meat. They are clothed like birds with wings for covering, they see no light, they sit in darkness. I entered the house of dust and I saw the kings of the earth, their crowns put away forever; rulers and princes, all those who once wore kingly crowns and ruled the world in the days of old. They who had stood in the place of the gods, like Anu and Enlil, stood now like servants to fetch baked meats in the house of dust, to carry cooked meat and cold water from the water-skin. . . . Then I awoke like a man drained of blood who wanders alone in a waste of rushes; like one whom the bailiff has seized and his heart pounds with terror.

Enkidu died, and Gilgamesh mourned the loss of his friend. Unable to face the fact of death, he went in search of eternal life. This search forms a major portion of the epic in which the hero met many trials and traveled to the ends of the earth. Upon meeting a wise woman, Gilgamesh told her of his search.

She answered, "Gilgamesh, where are you hurrying to? You will never find that life for which you are looking. When the gods created man they allotted to him death, but life they retained in their own keeping. As for you, Gilgamesh, fill your belly with good things; day and night, night and day, dance and be merry, feast and rejoice. Let your clothes be fresh, bathe yourself in water, cherish the little child that holds your hand, and make your wife happy in your embrace; for this too is the lot of man."

Gilgamesh continued his quest but to no avail. He pressed on, closer and closer to the abode of the gods, until he met *Utnapishtim*, the one mortal who, for some unknown reason, had been granted immortality. Utnapishtim told Gilgamesh of how he had attained this precious treasure. The tale he told is the story of a great flood.

In those days the world teemed, the people multiplied, the world bellowed like a wild bull, and the great god was aroused by the clamour. Enlil heard the clamour and he said to the gods in council, "The uproar of mankind is intolerable and sleep is no longer possible by reason of the babel." So the gods in their hearts were moved to let loose the deluge; but my lord Ea warned me in a dream. He whispered their words to my house of reeds, "Reed-house, reed-house! Wall, O wall, harken reed-house, wall reflect; O man of Shurrupak, son of Ubara-Tutu; tear down your house

Marburg—Art Reference Bureau

The strength and power of the epic hero Gilgamesh shows clearly in this colossal statue created by a Babylonian sculptor more than two thousand years ago.

and build a boat, abandon possessions and look for life, despise worldly goods and save your soul alive. Tear down your house, I say, and build a boat. These are the measurements of the barque as you shall build her: let her beam equal her length, let her deck be roofed like the vault that covers the abyss; then take up into the boat the seed of all living creatures."

Utnapishtim built the boat as directed.

Then was the launching full of difficulty; there was shifting of ballast above and below till two thirds was submerged. I loaded into her all that I had of gold and of living things, my family, my kin, the beasts of the field both wild and tame, and all the craftsmen. I sent them on board, for the time that Shamash had ordained was already fulfilled when he said, "In the evening, when the rider of the storm sends down the destroying rain, enter the boat and batten her down." The time was fulfilled, the evening came, the rider of the storm sent down the rain. I looked out at the weather and it was terrible, so I too boarded the boat and battened her down. All was now complete, the battening and the caulking; so I handed the tiller to Puzur-Amurri the steersman, with the navigation and the care of the whole boat.

With the first light of dawn a black cloud came from the horizon; it thundered within where Adad, lord of the storm, was riding. In front over hill and plain Shullat and Hanish, heralds of the storm, led on. Then the gods of the abyss rose up; Nergal pulled out the dams of the nether waters, Ninurta the war-lord threw down the dykes, and the seven judges of hell, the Annunaki, raised their torches, lighting up the land with their livid flame. A stupor of despair went up to heaven when the god of the storm turned daylight to darkness, when he smashed the land like a cup. One whole day the tempest raged gathering fury as it went, it poured over the people like the tides of battle; a man could not see his brother nor the people be seen from heaven. Even the gods were terrified at the flood, they fled to the highest heaven, the firmament of Anu; they crouched against the walls, cowering like curs. Then Ishtar the sweet-voiced Queen of Heaven cried out like a woman in travail: "Alas the days of old are turned to dust because I commanded evil; why did I command this evil in the council of the gods? I commanded wars to destroy the people, but are they not my people, for I brought them forth? Now like the spawn of fish they float in the ocean." The great gods of heaven and of hell wept, they covered their mouths.

For six days and six nights the winds blew, torrent and tempest and flood overwhelmed the world, tempest and flood raged together like warring hosts. When the seventh day dawned the storm from the south subsided, the sea grew calm, the flood was stilled; I looked at the face of the world and there was silence, all mankind was turned to clay. The surface of the sea stretched as flat as a roof-top; I opened a hatch and the light fell on my face. Then I bowed low, I sat down and I wept, the tears streamed down my face, for on every side was the waste of water. I looked for land in vain, but fourteen leagues distant there appeared a mountain, and there the boat grounded; on the mountain of Nisir the boat held fast, she held fast and did not budge. One day she held, and a second day on the mountain of Nisir she held fast and did not budge. . . . When the seventh day dawned I loosed a dove and let her go. She flew away, but finding no resting-place she returned. Then I loosed a swallow, and she flew away, but finding no resting-place she returned. I loosed a raven, she saw that the waters had retreated, she ate, she flew around, she cawed, and she did not come back. Then I threw everything open to the four winds, I made a sacrifice and poured out a libation on the mountaintop. Seven and again seven cauldrons I set up on their stands, I heaped up wood and cane and cedar and myrtle. When the gods smelled the sweet savour, they gathered like flies over the sacrifice. Then, at last, Ishtar also came, she lifted her necklace with the jewels of heaven that once Anu had made to please her. "O you gods here present, by the lapis lazuli round my neck I shall remember these days as I remember the jewels of my throat; these last days I shall not forget. Let all the gods gather round the sacrifice, except Enlil. He shall not approach this offering, for without reflection he brought the flood; he consigned my people to destruction."

. . . .

Utnapishtim said, "As for you, Gilgamesh, who will assemble the gods for your sake, so that you may find that life for which you are searching?"

This dramatic story was of little comfort to Gilgamesh, for great and wise as he was, he could not find eternal life. The land of the dead, as seen by Enkidu in his dream, was believed to be the fate of all Babylonians. Babylonian civilization did not have a belief in an afterlife, nor did it equip man with the ability to accept his fate. This spiritual tension produced a quality of creativity in Babylonian thought which was to influence later people.

This flood story may sound familiar to many people, and it should, because it is quite similar to the later story of Noah recorded in the Bible. There are, however, important differences between the two accounts.

In reality, the account of the flood may be based on fact. Since Mesopotamia was a land where floods were common, it is quite possible that a massive flood once did destroy most of the land. The memory of this great flood could well have survived through many generations by being passed down by word of mouth. Once the story was written down, it became a permanent part of civilization.

The Development of Astrology. In their attempt to understand the universe and the ways of the gods, the Babylonians looked to the heavens. They had once been pastoral people, tending their flocks by night, and so celestial bodies were important to them. Just as Paleolithic hunters had developed a vivid animal art and a totemistic religion, the Babylonians, from their exposure to the heavens, developed the practice of astrology. *Astrology* means, literally, knowledge of the stars; from this knowledge, the Babylonians thought that the course of human events could be predicted. Man and nature were part of the same substance, and so a natural occurrence in the heavens would have a direct effect on man. Astrology, invented by the Babylonians, was to remain an important element in man's intellectual culture. For example, the birth of Jesus was announced by means of a bright star; centuries later, the poet Shakespeare spoke of Romeo and Juliet as "star-crossed lovers," and even today, most newspapers have a section devoted to astrology.

In addition to seeking knowledge in the stars, the Babylonians thought that the insides of animals, especially the liver, would contain signs of things to come if interpreted correctly. This practice of seeking knowledge in the entrails of animals is called *divination*. The following Babylonian evening hymn shows not only the practice of divination but is in itself a fine example of the mythical view of the universe.

> They are lying down, the great ones.
> The bolts are fallen; the fastenings are placed.
> The crowds and people are quiet.
> The open gates are now closed.
> The gods and the goddesses of the land,
> Shamash, Sin, Adad, and Ishtar,
> Have betaken themselves to sleep in heaven.
> They are not pronouncing judgment;
> They are not deciding things.
> Veiled is the night;
> The temples and the most holy places are quiet and dark.
> The traveler calls on his god;
> And the litigant is tarrying in sleep.
> The judge of truth, the father of the fatherless,
> Shamash, has taken himself to his chamber.
> O Great Ones, gods of the night,
> O Bright one, Gibil, O warrior Irra,
> O bow (star) and yoke (star),
> O Pleiades, Orion and the dragon,
> O Ursa Major, goat (star) and the bison,
> Stand by, and then,
> In the divination which I am making,
> In the lamb which I am offering,
> Put truth for me.

This vision of night as something more than a revolution of the earth, in which the stars, sun and moon are living beings looking down upon the earth and speaking to man through the substance of another animal, is for us the realm of poetry, not of reality. For the ancient man, it was his reality, and in this sense, he may have led a more imaginative life than we do.

Around the middle of the second millennium, because of raids by barbarian tribesmen from the north and east, the Babylonian political structure eroded. For hundreds of years thereafter, Babylonia remained a minor power. In spite of the barbarian invasions, however, Babylonian civilization survived; in fact, it outlived the Babylonian empire. The civilization of Mesopotamia had reached its climax with the Babylonians. Borrowing and elaborating many

Sumerian ideas, the Babylonians provided a way of looking at man, society and the universe which was to last for centuries. Their laws provided the order needed for day-to-day life; their myths and stories expressed their beliefs about the nature of man as well as about the origin and structure of the universe. Many problems existed—they still do—but the Babylonians understood their world.

The Hittites

The tribesmen who invaded Babylonia came from Asia Minor and were called *Hittites*. Although the Hittites adopted much of Babylonian culture, they were not a Semitic people. This fact can be seen from their language. The Hittite language was a part of another ancient family of languages which is usually given the general name *Indo-European;* Greek, Latin and the modern languages of Europe are also members of the Indo-European family of languages. Even the language of ancient India—Sanskrit—is a member of this language group. Archaeologists now believe that during the early part of the second millennium, people speaking various Indo-European languages gradually migrated into India, the Middle East and as far west as present-day Europe. The rich lands and elaborate culture of the river valleys proved to be a constant temptation to underdeveloped people outside of this area.

Government. The Hittites, although they adopted many Babylonian forms of culture, began with their own distinct form of government which resulted, in part, from certain military factors. The Indo-European tribes were warriors who developed the technique of using horses to draw war chariots. This technological innovation gave them a great advantage over the more civilized river people who had used horses only for pulling carts and plows. Hittite society was dominated by those men who had the wealth to equip and maintain these new engines of war. These warriors grew into a kind of nobility which gained political power for itself.

The kings of the Hittites were the rulers of society, whose power rested not exclusively upon their unique relationship to the gods, but upon the support of their nobility, their chief warriors. Thus, the Hittites were ruled by a kind of monarchy in which the consent of the nobles was necessary if the king was to have any real power. Such a form of government might be called *feudalism,* and it was found in various forms among people with an Indo-European background. Although much of the feudal element in Hittite government disappeared as the Hittites adopted more and more Babylonian practices, this kind of government was an important factor in the development of lands occupied by Indo-Europeans. Its influence, for example, can be seen clearly during the so-called Middle Ages of our own Western history.

The Indo-Europeans who migrated closest to the Middle East, the Hittites, were the first to become civilized, whereas those who settled far to the west and north remained barbarians for centuries. (These western people were those later called Britons, Gauls and Germans.) The Hittites built a mighty nation in the second millennium B.C., rivaling that of the Egyptians, but during the next thousand years, they gradually disappeared as a separate group of people and were forgotten. That they had ever really existed was established only about sixty years ago by archaeologists digging in central Turkey.

Assimilation. Just how a culture "disappears" may be difficult to imagine. What happened was that the people were assimilated

Evidence of the warlike character of the Hittite people is this figure of a Hittite warrior, which was sculpted on a royal gateway about 1350 B.C.

Hirmer Fotoarchiv München

into cultures which were stronger and had the support of more people than theirs. The process is similar to that of groups of Europeans who come to the United States. A group of Frenchmen, for instance, might settle in the United States. After a few generations, this compact group of people practicing French culture gradually drops its French ways and, through disuse of its customs or intermarriage, develops American ways. In time, the Frenchmen "disappear"—not the people themselves but their Frenchness, their culture, which becomes absorbed into the more dominant American culture. Paul Revere, one of the patriots in colonial America, was the descendent of the Frenchman Revoir, whose family lost its Frenchness. In such a way did the Hittites, and many other cultural groups, "disappear" from history.

The Civilization of Crete

Another ancient civilization, the *Cretan,* which was almost as old as the Sumerian and Egyptian, also disappeared from history many centuries ago. The island of Crete is not far from Egypt. In the days before the development of good roads and efficient forms of land transportation, travel by sea was quick and economical. Even as recently as the American colonial period, the trip from Charlestown, South Carolina, to Boston was cheaper, faster and safer by ship than it was by land. It is not surprising, then, to find a civilization growing up at an early date on the island of Crete. There can be no doubt that civilized skills were transplanted from Egypt, but the cultural forms which grew on Crete have a distinctive style of their own.

Archaeological Evidence. Archaeology must lead the way in talking about Crete, for the written language of Crete is only now in the process of being translated. Until less than a hundred years ago, when archaeologists went to Crete, its civilization seemed never to have existed and had been mentioned only briefly by the Greeks, usually in their myths. The Greeks inhabited the shores of the Aegean Sea to the north of Crete after Cretan civilization had disappeared. A few myths told of this lost civilization, but until recently, myths were believed to contain no historical truth.

One of the "lost civilization" myths concerned Minos (MY nuhs), the king of Crete, who each year demanded from the citizens of Athens seven young men and seven young women as a tribute—a payment in recognition of the power which Crete had over the mainland. These young people then served as sacrificial

The archaeological discovery at Knossos included the palace throne room. Its elaborately decorated walls show the effects of time.

victims for the Minotaur—a beast with the body of a man and the head of a bull. The Greek hero Theseus (THEE see uhs) went down to Crete, killed the Minotaur, and then found his way out of the Cretan palace by following a string through a maze of small passageways. When archaeologists began excavation of the palace at Knossos (NAHS uhs) in Crete, they discovered that not only had the name Minos been given to Cretan rulers, but that the Cretans had worshipped a bull. They also discovered in the palace itself an elaborate drainage system resembling the maze through which Theseus was supposed to have escaped with the aid of his string. The civilization of Crete, remembered only in mythology, was in this way rediscovered.

Arts and Technology. From what has been found on this island, it seems that during the period 2000-1500 B.C., the kings of Crete ruled the Aegean Sea, exacting tribute from mainland dwellers and monopolizing the trade of the area. No significant literature from this culture has survived; its statuary, painting and architecture which have been found, however, are well developed. Cretan palaces, equipped with plumbing and lighting shafts, show a technical skill equal to that of any other civilized people. It is interesting to note that the Greek mythological figure Daedalus (DEAD uhluhs), a skilled craftsman, came from Crete.

Geographically, Crete is not a part of the Near East; in fact, Cretan civilization had its greatest impact on the Greeks, a European people. Crete is mentioned here because its civilization is almost as old as those of the Near East proper. Also, Crete acted as a connecting link between the Near East and the lands toward the west. The role played by the Cretans in the development and transmission of civilization is at present under intensive study by historians and archaeologists.

By now it should be clear that human culture can evolve along different lines in different places. Our knowledge of ancient civilizations is increasing all the time as more information is brought to light by the patient work of archaeologists. Yet, in spite of the spreading and changing of cultural forms in the second millennium B.C., the major centers of civilization remained the valleys of the rivers in Mesopotamia and Egypt. In this chapter, some aspects of Mesopotamian culture, drawn from its creative Babylonian period, have been presented. Egypt, which we will now look at again, is in many ways quite different, for the history of this civilization presents a long period of continuous and uninterrupted development. The age and mystery of Egypt was noticed by the ancients themselves, and the history of Egypt was already ancient history to the Greeks and Romans.

Define

Semitic	epic	Indo-European
codification	astrology	Minos
cosmogony	divination	Theseus

Review and Answer

1. Why was the development of *written* law a significant and necessary step in human civilization?
2. What does the Babylonian flood story tell us about Babylonian culture?
3. Is it possible to argue that Gilgamesh represented *man* as seen by the Babylonians?
4. What does the evening hymn (page 85) tell us about the Babylonian view of the universe?
5. Explain how a civilization "disappears."
6. How has the "truth" of a myth been confirmed by archaeological findings in Crete?

7

Imperial Egypt

The period of Egyptian history discussed in Chapter Five is called the Old Kingdom (2700-2200 B.C.). During subsequent centuries, the power of the central government declined, and the governors of local districts began to rule as separate princes. Although this period actually represented a decline in the pharaoh's power, the principle of a unified state ruled by a divine king never completely vanished. About the year 2000 B.C., the princes of the city of Thebes, located on the Nile in Upper Egypt, regained royal power and rebuilt the central government. This period is called the Middle Kingdom (2100-1788 B.C.). Around that time, Egypt was invaded by nomads who had been set into motion by the expanding Hittites. After a short occupation, Egypt became free, and an extensive empire was established. In spite of these political upheavals, the basic pattern of Egyptian life and culture remained fixed, and continued along the lines described in Chapter Five.

The Egyptian Mind

Egyptian civilization is difficult for us to understand because the Egyptian's view of man in relation to society and to the gods is so very different from ours. Egyptian polytheism, having so many gods with overlapping functions, tends to offend our way of thinking. For example, the pharaoh was the incarnation of Re, the sun god, as well as being the son of Re, but he was also Horus, the son of Osiris, and at times, he was Osiris himself. Horus could appear in the form of a bird or a baboon. A dead man had to be mummified so that the body would be preserved, permitting the ka to return to it, yet the man also went to eternal life, or was merged with the Nile or became a star. In many cases, he did all of these things. In our culture, all of our thinking is trained to seek a single coherent explanation for an event, and so the multiplicity of Egyptian thinking is almost impossible for us to comprehend.

For the Egyptians, however, the variety of answers merely showed a richness of thought. The pharaoh, as well as the other gods, could take many forms. Two or three explanations were better than one; if the universe was complex and varied, so should man's explanation of it be, if man was to be realistic. Various attempts were made by Egyptian thinkers to establish some kind of unity in religion, but they never succeeded. Even the myth of Osiris and Isis was never compiled in a single official version. We know of it mostly from the version organized by a Greek writer who lived after Egypt no longer existed as a separate state.

A Timeless Universe. For the Egyptians, the universe was static, time did not exist in the sense that we know it and nothing really changed. Nature moved in cycles—days, months, years—always repeating itself. The passage of years was dated not from a fixed event in the past, but from the beginning of the reign of each pharaoh. With each new king, the count began again. What we would call 1960 B.C., the Egyptians would call "the thirtieth year of the reign of Amen-emhet I." Perhaps it was the regular annual flooding of the Nile and the timelessness of the pyramids which gave the Egyptian his static view of the world. This static quality can be seen in Egyptian art, which retained a similar style throughout its three-thousand-year history, so that statues of different pharaohs look strangely similar. It was not the individual pharaoh that mattered; each one performed the same function, and so he was not portrayed as a distinct person.

Nature was always the same, and since there were no important changes, there was no sense of the past or of the future, only an eternal present. There was never a time when there was no pharaoh, and there would never be such a time. Perhaps this is why there is no significant Egyptian creation story, for that would indicate a period of time in which something had to be changed, in this case from nothing to something. It has been suggested that the Egyptian fascination with animals in art and religion comes from the fact that animals, unlike humans, do not change their physical appearance from generation to generation. If we were to ask an ancient Egyptian how long ago his civilization was founded, he would not only be unable to answer, he would find the question meaningless. Egyptians had no sense of history, Egypt had always been there. We have discovered no Egyptian account of their own history.

The Concept of Death. Death, of course, was a change, but here we find the Egyptians making a supreme effort to deny the fact of death. The elaborate process of mummification, designed to preserve the physical form of the body, is an example of this effort. The time and expense spent in ensuring the safe passage of the ka to the land of the dead shows the Egyptian desire to bridge the gap between life and death, making of it as little a change as possible. Hopefully, a person, once dead, would rejoin the cycle of nature, become united with Osiris and return each year with the Nile, the same way the pharaoh merged with the sun god to make his daily rounds. This desire to join with living nature and so to overcome the abrupt change of death accounts for the great fear the Egyptians had of not being properly buried. This fear is not lacking in our own modern culture. Shakespeare, in *Romeo and Juliet,* expressed what might well have been an Egyptian point of view when he said:

> When he shall die, take him and cut him out in little stars,
> And he will make the face of heaven so fine
> That all the world will be in love with night
> And pay no worship to the garish sun.

The Concept of Life. If death was a continuation of life, then life, the Egyptians thought, should be regulated by the rhythm of eternity, by the ordered structure of nature. Human values, the ideals of Egyptian life, bore the stamp of balance, order and regularity, imitating the cycle of nature into which a man eventually wished to return. Egyptian proverbs and wise sayings testify to this ordered view of ethical and social life. For example, in "The Instruction of the Vizer Ptah-Hotep," the teacher says to his son:

> Bow thy back to thy superior, the overseer from the palace. Then thy household will be established in its property, and thy recompense will be as it should be. Opposition to a superior is a painful thing, for one lives as long as he is mild.

Egyptian proverbs were not designed mainly to secure practical advantages by being nice to superiors; they also contained moral advice, as the following excerpt from "The Instruction of Amen-Hotep" shows.

> As for the heated man in the temple,
> He is like a tree growing in the open.

In the completion of a moment comes its
    loss of foliage,
And its end is reached in the shipyards;
Or it is floated far from its place,
    and the flame is its burial shroud.

But the truly silent man holds himself apart.
He is like a tree growing in a garden.
It flourishes and doubles its yield;
It stands before its lord.
Its fruit is sweet; its shade is pleasant,
And its end is reached in the garden.

Just what is meant in this excerpt by the "silent man" is difficult to say. Most likely, it should not be taken literally but rather refer to a man who is not excessive in his desires or violent in his treatment of others. This proverb is curiously similar in its message to that of the first psalm in the Hebrew Bible, and both pieces of wisdom stress the fact that good living brings its proper rewards.

During the long years of stable government and security from foreign attack, the ideals of Egyptian society were, perhaps, the

The most impressive example of Egyptian architecture and sculpture is the Temple of Amon-Re at Abu Simbel. Threatened by waters from the nearly completed Aswan High Dam, the 3200-year-old structure, weighing thousands of tons, was recently dismantled and moved to higher ground.

Wide World Photos

most cultivated of all times, with the values of the mind and spirit supplanting those of the fighting instincts. An example of these ideals is found in the following praise of learning from "The Instruction for King Merikere."

> Be a craftsman in thy speech so that thou mayest be strong, for the tongue is a sword to (a man), and speech is more valorous than any fighting. No one can circumvent the skillful of heart. . . . They who know his wisdom do not attack him and no (misfortune) occurs where he is. Truth comes to him (fully) brewed, in accordance with the sayings of the ancestors.

The "New" Pharaoh

The well-ordered society which we have seen develop in Egypt, ruled by a god-king who was supported by a hierarchy of people each staying in his proper place like the blocks of the pyramids, did not last forever. At the end of the Old Kingdom, when the central government lost its power, the pharaohs could no longer gain respect and obedience from religious devotion alone. The pyramids themselves were robbed of valuable contents and rulers had to become real rulers rather than religious symbols. King Merikere is here given some specific advice on the art of ruling.

> Advance thy great men so that they may carry out thy laws. He who is rich does not show partiality in his (own) house. He is a possessor of property who has no wants. (But) the poor man does not speak according to what is right for him. It is of no avail to say: "Would that I had!" He is partial to him who possesses rewards for him. Great is a great man when his great men are great. Valiant is the king possessed of courtiers; august is he who is rich in his nobles.

There is a good deal of political wisdom contained in this little proverb. How wise it actually is might well be debated, but it does indicate to us that the quality of Egyptian life was changing.

The Hyksos Invasion. Around the year 1600 B.C., Egyptian life changed rapidly when the country was invaded by the Hyksos, a nomadic people who came with horse-drawn war chariots. After several centuries of Hyksos rule, the invaders were expelled, leaving no significant mark upon Egyptian culture. The Hyksos invasion, did, however, make it necessary for the pharaohs to become warrior kings as well as religious leaders. The kings who came after the expulsion of the Hyksos ruled from the city of Thebes and ushered in the so-called Imperial Period (1580-1090 B.C.). They adopted some of the new techniques of war and began to build an Egyptian empire which soon stretched far into Syria. These kings no longer built pyramids but rather had their tombs cut into the cliffs which bordered the river near the city—the so-called Valley of the Kings.

The kings of the Eighteenth Dynasty, a family of pharaohs which ruled from 1580 to 1350 B.C., developed a large army and often led their men into battle, conquering new lands and bringing tribute and slaves back to Egypt. The city of Thebes grew rich, and many of the still-existing temples and statues date from this period. Cities in Syria fell under Egyptian rule, and the rich merchant cities along the coast of Syria, such as Byblos and Tyre, were compelled to supply the Egyptians with raw materials, especially timber from the forests of Lebanon.

The god associated with the city of Thebes was Amon (AH muhn); as Thebes rose to imperial power, Amon merged with Re, the sun god, to form the double deity Amon-Re. The king was still considered to be the son of Amon-Re, but most of his power rested on the strength and victories of his army. The priests gained more power as the pharaoh spent much of his time leading his armies into battle.

The Reign of Tutmosis III. Tutmosis III (1501-1447 B.C.) pushed the Egyptian empire to its greatest extent. The collapse of Hammurabi's kingdom in Babylon had left a vacuum in the Middle East, and the Egyptians moved in to gain control of the mountains of Syria, which could serve as a natural boundary from which to repel possible invasions. A decisive battle occurred at the Syrian city of Megiddo during the fifteenth century B.C. The exploits of Tutmosis at this battle were engraved on a wall in the temple of Karnak at Thebes, and a reading of them brings us close to the spirit of this period in Egyptian history.

> His majesty commanded that the victories which father Amon had given to him should be established upon a monument in the temple which his majesty had made for his father Amon in order to set down each individual campaign, together with the booty which his majesty carried off from it, and the dues of every foreign country which his father Re had given to him.
>
> His majesty set forth in a chariot of fine gold adorned with his accoutrements of combat like Horus the Mighty of Arm. . .while his father Amon made strong his arms. . . . Their horses and their chariots of gold and silver were captured as easy prey. Ranks of them were lying stretched out on their backs like fish in the bight of a net, while his majesty's victorious army counted up their

possessions. Now there was captured that wretched enemy's tent which was worked with silver.

Then the entire army rejoiced and gave praise to Amon because of this victory which he had given to his son on this day. They lauded his majesty and extolled his victories. Then they presented the plunder which they had taken; hands, living prisoners, horses and chariots of gold and silver and of painted work.

Now the princes of this foreign country came on their bellies to kiss the ground to the glory of his majesty and to beg breath for their nostrils because his arm was so great over every foreign country. . . . All of the princes whom the prowess of his majesty carried off, bearing their tribute of silver, gold, lapis lazuli and turquoise, and carrying grain, wine and large and small cattle for the army of his majesty, with one gang of them bearing tribute southward. Then his majesty appointed princes for every town. . . .

The inscription continues with a long list of the booty taken by the victorious army. This kind of pompous praise for "his majesty" shows how the Egyptian kings valued conquest and wished to have their praises sung loud and clear. These wars not only provided the basis for the great wealth of Egypt, but forced the Egyptians to move out of their isolation. War is a destructive thing, but it does often lead to the interchange of new ideas among those who survive. During the second millennium, the Egyptians came into contact with many different cultures, each of which had its own style of life and its own view of the universe. The cultural interchange which occurred caused some Egyptians to rethink their own beliefs, especially some of their religious beliefs. In the fourteenth century B.C., at the height of Egyptian imperial power, a serious attempt was made to reform Egyptian religion.

Religious Thought

The Atonist Movement. Amenhotep IV (ah muhn HOH tehp) came to the throne in 1375 B.C. He was a man lacking in physical strength and without a taste for war, but he had a sensitive spirit and an imaginative mind. What steps led him to his vision of one god are difficult to discover. Some historians say that he fostered his own religious ideas in order to break the power of the priests of Amon-Re. Other historians of Egypt, or Egyptologists as they are sometimes called, think that he wanted to have a single god which all of his new subjects could worship; the empire would then have religious as well as political unity. Perhaps he was just a thinker who grasped a sense of unity behind the polytheism of Egyptian religion and tried to make monotheism come about.

It has been suggested that since Amenhotep was not a good fighter, he turned his energies toward religious thought and attacked an idea. In his search for the one god, he looked to the sun, always an important element in Egyptian thought. The sun was a universal phenomenon, seen by all people. He called his sun god Aton (AH ton), and even changed his own name to Akhnaton (ahk NAHT uhn), which means "Aton is pleased." He tried to do away with the old gods, destroying their temples and priests and effacing their images throughout the land. He even built a new capital city to serve as the center of this new religion.

The best portrait of Akhnaton is a picture of him and his family worshipping the sun, with its rays spread out over the earth. It is in this picture that we can see, for the first time, a pharaoh portrayed as a human being, with all the irregular features of a distinct person, rather than as the official representation of the king—solid, imposing and always the same. With the Atonist movement, Egyptian thought and art seemed to be breaking its centuries old pattern and moving into new forms.

Yet the movement failed. It seemed as if the old gods had been around forever, and even the pharaoh himself was considered to be a god. A genuine monotheism cannot grow up if there is more than one divine personality, and the divinity of the pharaoh was difficult to change. Egyptian culture was too set in its ways, too frozen in the perfection of its balanced universe to make a radical change in religious thinking. Also, the cult of Aton was popular only in the close circle around the king and seemed to have little appeal to the masses of Egyptians. Most Egyptians were attracted more to the local gods or to the intensely human Osiris, together with his devoted wife and vigorous son, than they ever could be to a distant and abstract god such as Aton. Lacking mass support, the Atonist movement could not become a genuine revolution. The calmness and serenity of Aton as portrayed by the gentle pharaoh were miles apart from the imperious vigor of the Sumerian Enlil or the Babylonian Marduk. It might also be significant that Akhnaton, the religious reformer, died at an early age.

In any event, the Atonist movement collapsed with the death of Akhnaton. The priests revived the worship of the old gods; when the Hittites began to press upon the Egyptian empire, it seemed as if the gods of Egypt were punishing the land for this brief lapse in devotion to them. All that remains of the reform movement are

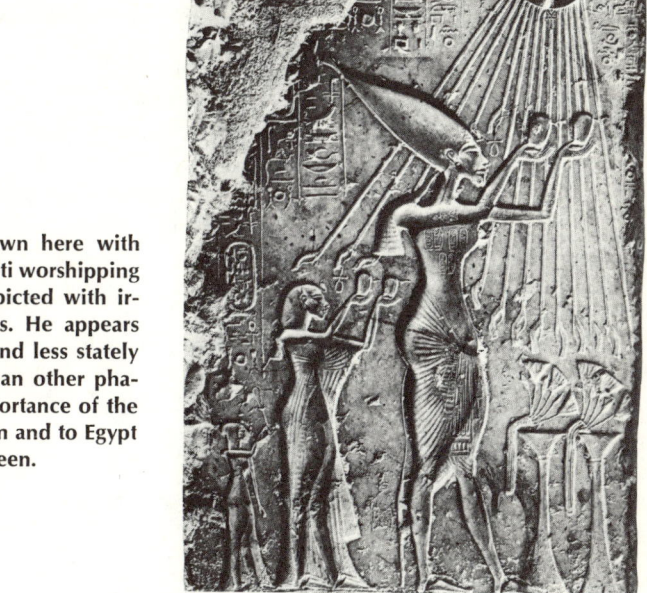

Akhnaton, shown here with his wife Nefretiti worshipping the sun, is depicted with irregular features. He appears more human and less stately and godlike than other pharaohs. The importance of the sun both to him and to Egypt can be clearly seen.

some striking works of art and a magnificent piece of religious poetry, the "Hymn to Aton."

The "Hymn to Aton." The "Hymn to Aton" is an example of the literary creativity which a nature religion can inspire. Even though this hymn represents an attempt to widen the scope of religious vision, it contains many deeply rooted Egyptian ideas. It can stand as an excellent summary of Egyptian civilization. Some sections of the hymn appear here.

> Thou appearest beautifully on the horizon of heaven,
> Thou living Aton, the beginning of life!
> When thou art risen on the eastern horizon,
> Thou has filled every land with thy beauty.
> Thou art gracious, great, glistening, and high over every land;
> Thy rays encompass the lands to the limit of all that thou
>   hast made:
> As thou art Re, thou reachest to the end of them;
> Thou subduest them for thy beloved son.
> Though thou art far away, thy rays are on earth;
> Though thou art in their faces, no one knows thy going.
>
> When thou settest in the western horizon,
> The land is in darkness, in the manner of death.
> They sleep in a room, with heads wrapped up,
> Nor sees one eye the other.
> All their goods which are under their heads might be stolen,

But they would not perceive it.
Every lion is come forth from his den;
All creeping things, they sting.
Darkness is a shroud, and the earth is in stillness,
For he who made them rests in his horizon.

At daybreak, when thou arisest on the horizon,
When thou shinest as the Aton by day,
Thou drivest away the darkness and givest thy rays.
The Two Lands are in festivity every day,
Awake and standing upon their feet,
For thou hast raised them up.
Washing their bodies, taking their clothing,
Their arms are raised in praise to thy appearance.
All the world, they do their work.

All beasts are content with their pasturage;
Trees and plants are flourishing.
The birds which fly from their nests,
Their wings are stretched out in praise to thy ka.
All beasts spring upon their feet.
Whatever flies and alights,
They live when thou hast risen for them.
The ships are sailing north and south as well,
For every way is open at thy appearance.
The fish in the river dart before thy face;
Thy rays are in the midst of the great green sea.

How manifold it is, what thou hast made!
They are hidden from the face of man.
O sole god, like whom there is no other!
Thou didst create the world according to thy desire,
Whilst thou wert alone:
All men, cattle and wild beasts,
Whatever is on earth, going upon its feet,
And what is on high, flying with its wings.

The countries of Syria and Nubia, the land of Egypt,
Thou settest every man in his place,
Thou suppliest their necessities:
Everyone has his food, and his time of life is reckoned.
Their tongues are separate in speech,
And their natures as well;
Their skins are distinguished,
As thou distinguishest the foreign peoples.
Thou makest a Nile in the underworld,
Thou bringest it forth as thou desirest
To maintain the people of Egypt
According as thou madest them for thyself,
The lord of all of them, wearying himself with them,
The lord of every land, rising for them
The Aton of the day, great of majesty.

All distant foreign countries, thou makest their life also,
For thou hast set a Nile in heaven,
That it may descend for them and make waves upon the mountains,
Like the great green sea,
To water their fields in their towns.
How effective they are, thy plans, O lord of eternity!
The Nile in heaven, it is for the foreign peoples
And for the beasts of every desert that go upon their feet;
While the true Nile comes from the underworld for Egypt.

The world came into being by thy hand,
According as thou hast made them.
When thou hast risen they live,
When thou settest they die,
Thou art lifetime thy own self,
For one lives only through thee.
Eyes are fixed on beauty until thou settest.
All work is laid aside when thou settest in the west.
But when thou risest again,
Everything is made to flourish for the king, . . .
Since thou didst found the earth
And raise them up for thy son,
Who came forth from thy body:
The King of Upper and Lower Egypt, . . . Akh-en-Aton, . . .
    and the Chief Wife of the King . . . Nefert-iti, living and
    youthful forever and ever.

    The kings who followed Akhnaton were warrior kings who brought Egypt to the final confrontation with the expanding Hittite empire. In the year 1285 B.C., near the Syrian city of Kadesh, a great battle was fought between these two empires. Neither side gained a decisive victory, and soon thereafter, a treaty was signed, with each empire agreeing to respect the territory of the other. A typical pharaoh of this period was Ramses II (RAM seez), whose statues, temples and tribute lists are impressive for their size and arrogance. Yet the Egyptian empire had reached the limits of its expansion. The pharaohs could no longer count on the religious devotion of their people to build the great monuments but rather had to employ slave labor. It was during the reign of Ramses II that a small group of Asiatics who had been residing in Egypt decided to flee the country so as to escape the harsh rule of the Egyptian government. These people were called the Hebrews, and their departure, so significant an event for later culture, was not even mentioned in Egyptian records.
    It is quite possible that the Hebrews were living in Egypt during the reign of the pharaoh Akhnaton. A few historians suggest that some of the religious ideas found in the Hebrew culture drew

their inspiration from Akhnaton's beliefs. A number of Egyptologists would like to show that the ideas underlying the Atonist movement lived on after the death of Akhnaton. Historians today, however, are still not agreed on the influence of this movement.

Egypt and Mesopotamia were the two birthplaces of civilization —"the cradles of civilization," as they are sometimes called. Egypt attained a stately quality of religion and literature and a monumental grandeur as seen in its pyramids. Mesopotamian civilization was less stable. Its temples and cities were buried in the sands of the desert, and its religion and literature had a restless and striving quality to it. Comparing the Babylonian creation story and the "Hymn to Aton," and looking at the adventures of both Sinuhe and Gilgamesh, we might gain a sense of the different nature of each civilization.

Which of these two ancient civilizations was greater? The answer might well depend upon a person's temperament. As we move into the next period of the history of the Near East, we must keep the legacy of both Egypt and Mesopotamia in mind as we witness new people and new ideas moving into our range of historical vision.

Define

Hyksos   Aton
Tutmosis III   Akhnaton

Review and Answer

1. How do ancient Egyptian patterns of thought differ from our own, particularly in the concept of time?
2. Explain what the following idea means: "Great is the great man when his great men are great."
3. What is a precise definition of "empire"? What were the reasons for the development of the Egyptian empire?
4. What reasons could be given for the failure of Akhnaton's idea of monotheism?
5. If the "Hymn to Aton" is "a summary of Egyptian civilization," how much about Egypt and the Egyptians can be learned from a close reading of it?
6. Give some specific facts to illustrate the concept of balance and harmony in ancient Egyptian thought.

Reading III

The cuneiform tablet containing Hammurabi's Code was discovered by a French archaeologist in 1901. With this discovery, historians acquired a major source of information about the social structure and legal system of ancient Mesopotamian society. This collection of laws is a treasury of evidence from which many conclusions about early civilization can be made, more than we may think at first. Listed below are thirty-four laws, selected from the entire collection of 282, dealing with many aspects of Babylonian culture.

We have the opportunity here to be our own historians, composing a picture of Babylonian life by using these laws as evidence and interpreting them as we see fit. Not only should we be able to discover what kinds of things the Babylonians did or knew how to do, but we will have to make some evaluation of their legal and ethical values. We might have some strong reactions to some of these laws, but we should try to be as objective as possible. A lot of reading is not necessary, but a good deal of thinking is. Any one of these laws will tell us much about this ancient society if we apply some intelligence and imagination to the task.

The Code of Hammurabi

When lofty Anu, king of the Anunnaki, and Enlil, lord of heaven and earth, the determiner of the destinies of the land, determined for Marduk, the first born of Enki, the Enlil functions over all mankind, made him great among the Igigi, called Babylon by its exalted name, made it supreme in the world, established for him in its midst an enduring kingship, whose foundations are as firm as heaven and earth—
At that time Anu and Enlil named me to promote the welfare of the people, me, Hammurabi, the devout, god-fearing prince, to cause justice to prevail in the land, to destroy the wicked and evil, that the strong might not oppress the weak, to rise like the sun over the black-headed people and to light up the land. . . . I established law and justice in the language of the land, thereby promoting the welfare of the people. At that time I decreed:

(1) If a man accused another and brought a charge of murder against him, but has not proved it, his accuser shall be put to death.

(2) If a man brought a charge of sorcery against another man, but has not proved it, the one against whom the charge of sorcery was brought, upon going to the river, shall throw himself into the river, and if the river has then overpowered him, his accuser shall take over his estate; if the river has shown that man to be innocent and he has accordingly come forth safe, the one who brought the charge of sorcery against him shall

---

T.J. Meek, trans., in J.B. Pritchard, ed., *Ancient Near Eastern Texts Relating to the Old Testament* (Princeton: Princeton University Press, 1955), pp. 164-177, *et passim*. Reprinted by permission of Princeton University Press.

be put to death, while the one who threw himself into the river shall take over the estate of the accuser.

(3) If a man came forward with false testimony in a case, and has not proved the word which he spoke, if that case was a case involving life, that man shall be put to death.

(5) If a judge gave a judgement, rendered a decision, deposited a sealed document, but later has altered his judgement, they shall prove that the judge altered the judgement which he gave and he shall pay twelve-fold the claim which holds in that case; furthermore they shall expel him in the assembly from the seat of judgement and he shall never again sit with the judges in a case.

(8) If a man stole either an ox, or a sheep, or an ass, or a pig, or a boat if it belonged to the church or if it belonged to the state, he shall make thirty-fold restitution; if it belonged to a private citizen, he shall make good ten-fold. If the thief does not have sufficient to make restitution, he shall be put to death.

(16) If a man has harbored in his house either a fugitive male or female slave belonging to the state or to a private citizen and has not brought him forth at the summons of the police, that householder shall be put to death.

(21) If a man made a breach in a house, they shall put him to death in front of that breach and wall him in.

(22) If a man committed robbery and has been caught, that man shall be put to death.

(23) If the robber has not been caught, the robbed man shall set forth the particulars regarding his lost property in the presence of god, and the city and governor, in whose territory and district the robbery was committed, shall make good to him his lost property.

(24) If it was a life that was lost, the city and governor shall pay one mina of silver to his people.

(32) If a merchant has ransomed either a private soldier or an officer who was carried off in the campaign of the king, and has enabled him to reach his city, if there is sufficient to ransom him in his house, he himself shall ransom himself; if there is not sufficient to ransom him in his house, he shall be ransomed from the estate of his city-god; if there is not sufficient to ransom him in the estate of his city-god, the state shall ransom him, since his own field, orchard and house may not be given for his ransom.

(36) In no case is the field, orchard, or house belonging to a soldier ... salable.

(42) If a man rented a field for cultivation, but has not produced grain in the field, they shall prove that he did not work on the field and he shall give grain to the owner of the field on the basis of those adjoining it.

(48) If a debt is outstanding against a man and (a storm) has inundated his field or a flood has ravaged it, or through lack of water grain has not been produced in the field, he shall not make any return of grain to his creditor in that year; he shall cancel his contract-tablet and he shall pay no interest for that year.

(104) If a merchant lent grain, wool, oil, or any goods at all to a trader to retail, the trader shall write down the value and pay it back to the merchant, with the trader obtaining a sealed receipt for the money which he pays to the merchant.

(105) If the trader has been careless and so has not obtained a sealed receipt for the money which he paid to the merchant, the money with no sealed receipt may not be credited to the account.

(109) If outlaws have congregated in the establishment of a woman wine seller and she has not arrested those outlaws and did not take them to the palace, that wine seller shall be put to death.

(121) If a man stored grain in another man's house, he shall pay five *qu* of grain per *kur* of grain as the storage-charge per year.

(128) If a man acquired a wife, but did not draw up the contracts for her, that woman is not his wife.

(138) If a man wishes to divorce his wife who did not bear him children, he shall give her money to the full amount of her marriage-price and he shall also make good to her the dowry which she brought from her father's home and then he may divorce her.

(168) If a man, having made up his mind to disinherit his son, has said to the judges, "I wish to disinherit my son," the judges shall investigate his record, and if the son did not incur wrong grave enough to be disinherited, the father may not disinherit his son.

(188) If a member of the artisan class took a son as a foster child and has taught him his handicraft, he may never be reclaimed.

(189) If he has not taught him his handicraft, that foster child may return to his father's house.

(195) If a son has struck his father, they shall cut off his hand.

(196) If a man has destroyed the eye of a member of the aristocracy, they shall destroy his eye.

(197) If he has broken another man's bone, they shall break his bone.

(198) If he has destroyed the eye of a commoner or broken the bone of a commoner, he shall pay one mina of silver.

(199) If he has destroyed the eye of a man's slave or broken the bone of a man's slave, he shall pay one-half his value.

(202) If a man has struck the cheek of a man who is superior to him, he shall be beaten sixty times with an oxtail whip in the assembly.

(215) If a physician performed a major operation on a man with a bronze lancet and has saved the man's life, or he opened up the eye-socket of a man with a bronze lancet and has saved the man's eye, he shall receive ten shekels of silver.

(216) If it was a commoner, he shall receive five shekels.

(218) If a physician performed a major operation on a man with a bronze lancet and has caused the man's death, or he opened up the eye-socket of a man and has destroyed the man's eye, they shall cut off his hand.

(237) When a man hired a boatman and a boat and loaded it with grain, wool oil, dates, or any kind of freight, if that boatman was so careless that he has sunk the boat and lost what was in it as well, the boatman shall make good the boat which he sank and whatever he lost that was in it.

(282) If a male slave has said to his master, "You are not my master," his master shall prove him to be his slave and cut off his ear.

The stele on which Hammurabi's Code is written shows him on a mountaintop standing before the sun god, from whom he received the laws.

The Louvre

Reading IV

This myth is perhaps the most elaborate cosmogony of the ancient world. The creation myth was recited by the Babylonian priests at the New Year's festival each year to celebrate the creation of the world and to sing the praises of Marduk, the major Babylonian god.

The portion of the myth given here tells first of the choice of Marduk by the high gods to perform the acts of creation. Marduk's struggle with chaos, represented by the goddess Tiamat, is then described. Finally, Marduk creates the heavenly bodies, earth and man himself.

The story is told with dramatic effect and vivid detail, and it illustrates quite well the mythological view of the universe. Chaos is portrayed as a person, and the universe itself is made out of the substance of the goddess Tiamat. In reading this myth, note the importance given to the moon and the way in which mankind is created.

The Babylonian Creation Story

They erected for him a princely throne
Facing his fathers, he sat down presiding.
"Thou are the most honored of the great gods,
Thy decree is unrivaled, thy command is Anu.
Thou, Marduk, art the most honored of the great gods,
Thy decree is unrivaled, thy word is Anu.
From this day unchangeable shall be thy pronouncement
To raise or bring low—these shall be in thy hand.
Thy utterance shall be true, thy command shall be unimpeachable.
No one among the gods shall transgress thy bounds!

Adornment being wanted for the seats of the gods,
Let the place of their shrines be ever in thy place.
O Marduk, thou art indeed our avenger.
We have granted thee kingship over the universe entire.
When in Assembly thou sittest, thy word shall be supreme.
Thy weapons shall not fail; they shall smash thy foes!
O lord, spare the life of him who trusts thee,
But pour out the life of the god who seized evil."

Having placed in their midst a piece of cloth,
They addressed themselves to Marduk, their first-born:
"Lord, truly thy decree is first among the gods.
Say but to wreck or create; it shall be.
Open thy mouth: the cloth will vanish!
Speak again, and the cloth shall be whole!"

E.A. Speiser, trans., in J.B. Pritchard, ed., *Ancient Near Eastern Texts Relating to the Old Testament* (Princeton: Princeton University Press, 1955), pp. 66-68. Reprinted by permission of Princeton University Press.

At the word of his mouth the cloth vanished.
He spoke again, and the cloth was restored.
When the gods, his fathers, saw the fruit of his word,
Joyfully they did homage: "Marduk is king!"
They conferred on him scepter, throne and vestment;
They gave him matchless weapons that ward off the foes:
"Go and cut off the life of Tiamat.
May the winds bear her blood to places undisclosed."

Bel's destiny thus fixed, the gods, his fathers,
Caused him to go the way of success and attainment.
He constructed a bow, marked it as his weapon,
Attached thereto the arrow, fixed its bow-cord.
He raised the mace, made his right hand grasp it;
Bow and quiver he hung at his side.
In front of him he set the lightning,
With a blazing flame he filled his body.
He made a net to enfold Tiamat therein.
The four winds he stationed that nothing of her might
    escape.
The South Wind, the North Wind, the East Wind, the
    West Wind.
Close to his side he held the net, the gift of his father
    Anu.
He brought forth Imhullu "The Evil Wind," the Whirlwind,
    the Hurricane.
The Fourfold Wind, the Sevenfold Wind, the Cyclone,
    the Matchless Wind;
Then he sent forth the winds he had brought forth, the
    seven of them.
To stir up the inside of Tiamat they rose up behind him.

Then the lord raised up the flood-storm, his mighty weapon.
He mounted the storm-chariot irresistible and terrifying.
He harnessed and yoked it to a team-of-four,
The Killer, the Relentless, the Trampler, the Swift.
Sharp were their teeth, bearing poison.
They were versed in ravage, in destruction skilled.
On his right he posted the Smiter, fearsome in battle,
On the left the Combat, which repels all the zealous.
For a cloak he was wrapped in an armor of terror;
With his fearsome halo his head was turbaned.
The lord went forth and followed his course,
Towards the raging Tiamat he set his face.
In his lips he held a spell;
A plant to put out poison was grasped in his hand.
Then they milled about him, the gods milled about him,
The gods, his fathers, milled about him, the gods milled
    about him.

The lord approached to scan the inside of Tiamat,
And of Kingu, her consort, the scheme to perceive.
As he looks on, his course becomes upset.
His will is distracted and his doings are confused.
And when the gods, his helpers, who marched at his side,
Saw the valiant hero, blurred became their vision.
Tiamat emitted a cry, without turning her neck,
Framing savage defiance in her lips.

. . . .

"Stand thou up that I and thou meet in single combat!"
When Tiamat heard this,
She was like one possessed; she took leave of her senses.
In fury Tiamat cried aloud.
To the roots her legs shook both together.
She recites a charm, keeps casting her spell,
While the gods of battle sharpen their weapons.
Then joined issue, Tiamat and Marduk, wisest of Gods.
They strove in single combat, locked in battle.
The lord spread out his net to enfold her,
The Evil Wind, which followed behind, he let loose in her face.
When Tiamat opened her mouth to consume him,
He drove in the Evil Wind that she close not her lips.
As the fierce winds charged her belly,
Her body was distended and her mouth was wide open.
He released the arrow, it tore her belly,
It cut through her insides, splitting the heart.
Having thus subdued her, he extinguished her life.

He cast down her carcass to stand upon it.
After he had slain Tiamat, the leader,
Her band was shattered, the troupe broken up;
And the gods, her helpers who marched at her side,
Trembling with terror, turned their backs about,
In order to save and preserve their lives.
Tightly encircled they could not escape.
He made them captives and he smashed their weapons.
Thrown into the net, they found themselves ensnared;
Placed in cells, they were filled with wailing;
Bearing his wrath, they were held imprisoned. . . .

The lord trod on the legs of Tiamat,
With his unsparing mace he crushed her skull.
When the arteries of her blood he had severed,
The North Wind bore it to the places undisclosed.
On seeing this, his fathers were joyful and jubilant,
They brought the gifts of homage, they to him.
Then the lord paused to view her dead body,

That he might divide the monster and do artful works.
He split her like a shellfish into two parts:
Half of her he set up and ceiled it as the sky,
Pulled down the bar and posted guards.
He bade them to allow not her waters to escape. . . .

He constructed stations for the great gods,
Fixing their astral likenesses as constellations.
He determined the year by designating the zones:
He set up three constellations for each of the twelve months.
After defining the days of the years by means of heavenly figures,
He founded the station of Nebiru to determine their heavenly bands.
That none might transgress or fall short. . . .
In her belly he established the zenith.
The Moon he caused to shine, the night to him entrusting.
He appointed him a creature of the night to signify the days:
"Monthly without cease, form designs with a crown.
At the month's very start, rising over the land,
Thou shalt have luminous horns to signify six days,
On the seventh day reaching a half crown.
At full moon stand in opposition in mid-month.
When the sun overtakes thee at the base of heaven,
Diminish thy crown and retrogress in light.
At the time of disappearance approach thou the course of the sun,
And on the twenty-ninth thou shalt again stand in opposition to the sun."

When Marduk hears the words of the gods,
His heart prompts him to fashion artful works.
Opening his mouth he addresses Ea
To impart the plan he had conceived in his heart:
"Blood will I mass and cause bone to be.
I will establish a savage, 'man' shall be his name.
Verily savage-man I will create.
He shall be charged with the service of the gods that they might be at ease.
The ways of the gods I will artfully alter.
Though alike revered, into two groups they shall be divided."
Ea answered him, speaking a word to him,
Giving him another plan for the relief of the gods:
"Let but one of their brothers be handed over;
He alone shall perish that mankind may be fashioned.
Let the great gods be here in Assembly,
Let the guilty be handed over that they may endure."

THE BABYLONIAN CREATION STORY

Marduk summoned the great gods to Assembly;
Presiding graciously, he issues instructions. . . .
"Who was it that contrived the uprising,
And made Tiamat rebel, and joined battle?
Let him be handed over who contrived the uprising.
His guilt I will make him bear. You shall dwell in peace!"
The Igigi, the great gods, replied to him . . . ,
"It was Kingu who contrived the uprising,
And made Tiamat rebel, and joined battle."
They bound him, holding him before Ea.
They imposed on him his guilt and severed his blood vessels.
Out of his blood they fashioned mankind.

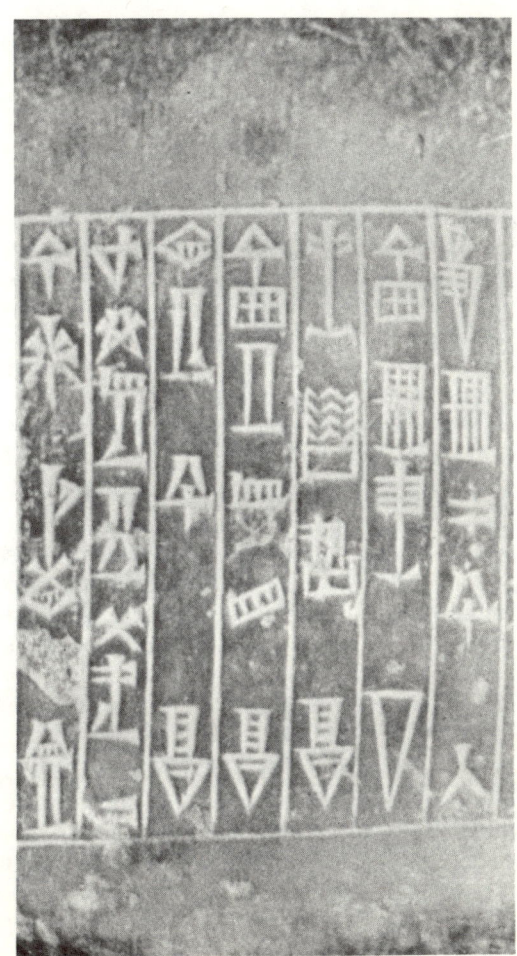

The Babylonian creation story was written in cuneiform symbols, as shown here. Many more works of literature may still exist on tablets buried in the sands of the Near East.

Around the middle of the second millennium B.C., the stability of the Near East was broken. New people, less civilized than those living in or near the river valleys, moved into the area more rapidly than they had ever done before. The sea of barbarians which lay to the north and east of the Near East was spilling over into the inviting lands to the south. The Hittite empire was so overwhelmed that its culture disappeared entirely from recorded history. Raiders from the sea broke the Egyptian hold on the Syrian coastal cities and attacked even Egypt itself. Tribes of Indo-Europeans moved into Greece, overran the island of Crete and brought about many changes.

This rapid overflowing of the barbarian reservoir started a chain of migrations. One group of people called Philistines moved by sea to the coast of Syria and settled in a land which they called Philistia. The land was later to be called Palestine. Tribes of Indo-Europeans called Hellenes (later to be called Greeks) moved into Greece and destroyed what civilization was there. Pastoral people with a Semitic background, called Hebrews, moved into central Palestine and conquered the more civilized inhabitants. The migration of peoples into good farming lands disrupted government and often lowered the level of culture.

Yet, a large-scale mixing of men and ideas can often lead to change and progress. New ideas, some of them revolutionary, were born during this period and carried far and wide. In time, stability was regained and with it came new governments capable of imposing their rule over large areas. By the middle of the first millennium, civilization had spread well beyond the Middle East, and the number of different groups of people had increased.

UNIT IV
The Spread of Civilization

8

The Small Nations

The period following the twelfth century B.C. had several main characteristics: (1) large empires declined, (2) many more groups of people developed and (3) the historical process speeded up. This period appeared to be a kind of "dark ages" in which the less civilized people seemed to gain the upper hand. Yet, during this period, man developed new ideas, thereby increasing the scope of civilization.

The Discovery of Iron

Before looking at some specific people and their accomplishments, we must note one significant invention, a technological advance which brought about a revolution. This revolution was not the kind which topples kings from power and sends rioters running through the streets to overthrow the government. Rather, it was a revolution much like the Neolithic Revolution—one which occurred slowly but which brought about a basic change in human society and culture. We know about some of the changes which were based on the once-new technology of farming and herding. We must now look at the Iron Age Revolution, which was based on the discovery and production of a special kind of metal.

During the fifteenth century B.C., an unknown tribe somewhere in the mountains of Armenia discovered how to smelt iron ore, one of earth's most common minerals. By 1200 B.C., iron tools and weapons were being introduced to the world, not by the civilized peoples but by barbarians who had mastered the process. It is important to note that this invention was brought about by people not living in the civilized areas of the world.

Until this time, man had relied on bronze, an alloy of copper and tin. These two minerals are not as plentiful as iron; therefore, bronze weapons and tools remained in small supply. Consequently, armies consisted of a small number of bronze-armed warriors supported by masses of poorly armed or totally unarmed peasants. Because of this limited supply of weapons, the majority of the population of any nation could not be effectively armed. Warfare usually consisted of a duel between the nobility of each army. Bronze provided an excellent basis for a society led by a few.

Iron, on the other hand, could not only be produced in greater quantity, but it was much stronger than bronze. Because of these characteristics of iron, its extensive use brought about two significant results. First, more land could be plowed with the stronger tools and the food supply thereby increased. Also, land which had previously been unfarmable could now be brought under cultivation. Civilization now had the economic basis to spread into lands not blessed by a fertile river valley. Second, the use of iron made it possible for the entire population of a land to be armed with excellent weapons. This fact brought about a political and social revolution. Barbarian tribes with their armed peasantry were militarily superior to the more civilized nations which had a bronze-armed nobility and unarmed peasants.

The old "bronze empires" could not readily alter their society and turn their peasantry into an effective army. As a result, the balance of power shifted. The Bronze Age had ended and so had the predominance of the river valleys. Societies of men on the fringes of the Near East now possessed the technology to become civilized and to challenge the ancient seats of culture. The discovery of iron might well explain why barbarian peoples were able to invade the civilized areas with such ease. The period of the invasions might look like a "dark age," but iron was ultimately to provide the economic power with which to advance the spread of civilization. The discovery of iron was similar to the recent discovery of atomic energy. It has been used to destroy, but the power of the atom carries with it the hope of a richer life for many people.

Phoenicia and the Alphabet

One area of the Near East which became important during the early Iron Age was the land between Egypt and Mesopotamia.

This area is sometimes called Syria-Palestine. It had once been the meeting place of Egyptian and Mesopotamian cultures as well as the battleground of Egyptian and Hittite armies. Syria-Palestine was inhabited by a number of different peoples grouped together in small separate states rather than in a large nation.

A Nation of Traders. One important people in this area were the Phoenicians, a seafaring folk who lived in and around the coastal cities of Tyre, Sidon and Byblos. When Egypt had been powerful, these cities had been under the rule of the pharaohs and had paid tribute to the rulers of the Nile. With the decline of Egyptian imperial power, these cities came into their own and became wealthy seaports, sending merchants and settlers to the far reaches of the Mediterranean Sea.

As traders, the Phoenicians acted as middlemen between civilized and barbarian peoples. The Phoenicians founded faraway cities called *colonies*, which acted as civilized outposts in a barbarian world. Most of these cities were on the northern coast of Africa, the most important being the city of Carthage on the site of modern-day Tunis. Carthage, a rich commerical city, had a powerful empire of its own and remained a major center of civilization in the western Mediterranean until it was destroyed by the Romans many centuries later. The city of Cadiz in Spain was another Phoenician colony. This port acted as a stopping-off point for the Phoenician ships going into the ocean through the Strait of Gibraltar. It is believed that much of the tin used in the ancient world came from mines on the island of Britain. Phoenician traders carried this product to the Near East.

In addition to being the carriers of goods, the Phoenicians had a product which was very valuable in the ancient world. From certain kinds of shellfish, they extracted a pigment which was used to make a purple dye for coloring fabrics. This purple dye was the only kind of artificial coloring available in the ancient world. For this reason, purple was worn by kings to distinguish them from the rest of the people. Wherever there are kings, even today, purple is the color associated with them.

The Phoenicians spoke a Semitic language similar to that of the Babylonians, and their religion contained the mythological beliefs which had been established for centuries. However, they have been credited with one highly significant invention, a discovery perhaps as important as the discovery of iron. To the best of our knowledge, the Phoenicians invented the alphabet.

The Alphabet. Writing, of course, had been invented over two thousand years before by the Sumerians and Egyptians. Their kind of writing was pictographic in form, a style of writing in which actual pictures of an idea or item were drawn. Over the years, pictographic writing was simplified by having one picture stand for several things. Also, certain pictures could stand for sounds, for example, a bee for the "b" sound. This was a kind of alphabet of sounds, although the concept of writing as a collection of pictures still remained. In spite of these simplifications, pictographic writing was a difficult art to learn. The actual writing was an art in itself; a writer was also an artist bringing his own particular touches to each picture. Each man's writing was, in a sense, a separate work of art, and much of the richness of visual experience could be captured in written documents.

Alphabetic writing is quite different. It is unartistic and uniform. Once the concept of letters was grasped, each letter had no meaning in itself, and the act of writing was no longer an art. The basic number of letters, usually no more than thirty, could be combined into an infinite number of arrangements to form words. Each word carried with it no visual significance as picture-writing had done. Alphabetic writing was and is much like a code with agreed upon rules for the joining of letters into words. Whether this is a better form of writing is a debatable point. Many medieval manuscripts have elaborate designs drawn around opening letters. Could this practice indicate a desire to return to the artistic richness of pictographic writing?

The Egyptians and Babylonians got along with pictographs for centuries, and today the Chinese do not use an alphabet. Nonetheless, alphabetic writing is easier to learn. The basic letters can be mastered by a child of four, and from this level, a person can become literate with comparative ease. The social and political consequences of this fact should be clear at once. To learn pictographic writing requires years of study, and so the class of scribes and priests could have a monopoly of the power which literacy brings. Using an alphabet, a greater number of people could gain the skill of reading and writing. With this powerful instrument of human communication in the hands of many, the rule of a few was no longer assured. High positions were open to more people, and rapid social change could take place. More people could rise to power, and more people could record their thoughts. The base of civilization became broader.

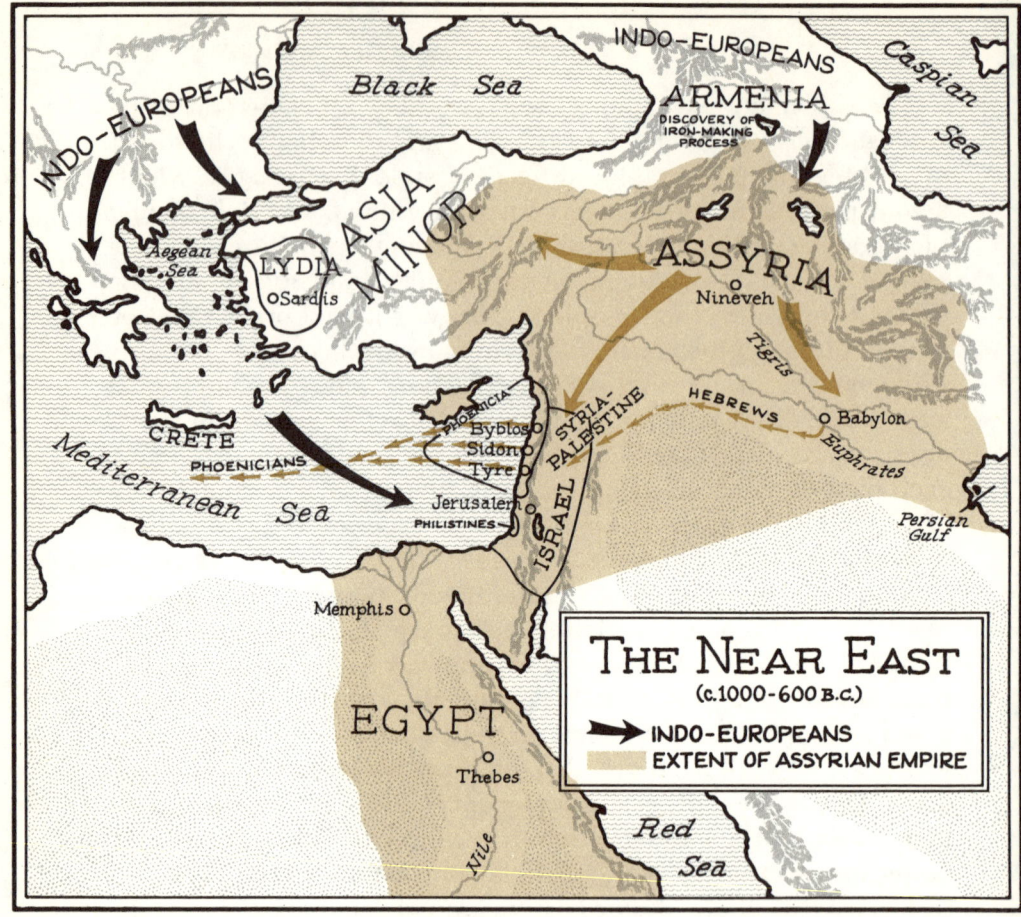

After their conquest of the small states in Syria-Palestine, the Assyrians moved west, overrunning Egypt in the late 600's B.C.

Pictographic writing also tended to separate different peoples from each other because each culture had different symbols and pictures. With the coming of the alphabet, translation became easier, and cultural barriers began to break down. Different languages still existed, as they do today, but they were all written with similar letters. Ideas could spread among different peoples more rapidly than ever before, and the civilized area began to increase. The alphabet, like iron, was an efficient machine for the building and spreading of civilization.

Because of this increase in literacy, the written evidence of history increased. Therefore, as we move into the first millennium B.C., the historian has more material from which to build his picture of the past. Pictographic writing did not disappear with the invention of the alphabet, but this new form of communication was the way of the future. Picture writing, a beautiful and subtle means of communication, gradually died out in most of the world. Whether civilization has profited from this change is difficult to say.

Regardless of how we choose to regard the alphabet, we must admit that the Phoenicians emerged from the turmoil of the early Iron Age and played an important role in the development of civilization. Through their overseas trade, they carried the arts of civilization far beyond the Near East, and through the alphabet, they gave a new dimension to human culture.

Canaan and the Dying God

The Phoenicians were not the only people to inhabit the land called Syria-Palestine. On the fertile strip in the interior of Palestine, a group of people called Canaanites developed a culture of their own. Because of them, this land is sometimes referred to as the land of Canaan. These people had the advantage of living midway between the valleys of the Nile and Euphrates, and so they profited from both Egyptian and Mesopotamian civilization. They were also near enough to the sea to come into contact with people living outside the Near East. Semitic and Indo-European peoples moved through this land, Hittites as well as Egyptians and Babylonians. When the empires of Tutmosis in Egypt and Hammurabi in Babylonia were strong, this land was submerged beneath the great powers. However, during the early Iron Age, the big empires were no longer there, and the cities of Canaan flourished. The Hebrews who migrated there as rude shepherds called it a "land of milk and honey."

The Canaanites were an agricultural people, and their religious beliefs and practices were similar to those of other agricultural people. The names of their gods were different from those of the Egyptians or Sumerians, but these gods performed the same functions; they were gods of nature. Being dependent on the soil and on the changing seasons, the religion of the Canaanites focused on the source of their livelihood. Just as the Babylonians worshipped the goddess Ishtar who descended into the earth and returned with crops, the people of Canaan worshipped gods of fertility.

Their most important myth was that of Baal (BAY uhl) and his female counterpart Anat (AH naht). Each year, Baal was captured and separated from his partner by Mot, the god of the underworld. Through the efforts of Anat, Baal was restored to life, and with his resurrection, the fertility of the soil returned. Needless to say, this myth represents the same basic theme as does the Egyptian myth of Isis and Osiris.

In the Near East, fall and winter are the rainy seasons when the seed is planted. During the dry summer, no food can grow. This fact of nature is portrayed in the fragment of the Baal myth which follows. Baal represents the wet, fertile season; Mot represents the dry, infertile season.

> As the heart of a cow toward her calf,
> As the heart of a ewe toward her lamb,
> So is the heart of Anat for Baal.
> She seizes Mot by the fold of his robe,
> Grasps him by the edge of his garment.
> She lifts up her voice and cries:
>
> "Thou, Mot, give me back my brother!"
>
> But the god Mot makes answer:
>
> "What wouldst thou, O maiden Anat? . . .
> I met the mighty Baal,
> And made him as a lamb in my mouth,
> Like a kid in my throat was he crushed."
>
> A day passes, and two days,
> And after the days, the months.
> Maiden Anat draws near to him.
> As the heart of the cow toward her calf,
> As the heart of a ewe toward her lamb,
> So is the heart of Anat for Baal.
> She seizes the god Mot;
> With sword she cleaves him,
> With fan she winnows him,
> With fire she burns him,
> With mill she grinds him,
> In the fields she sows him,
> Birds eat the pieces of him,
> Devour the bits of him.

After the destruction of Mot—the destruction of the dry summer—Baal returns, and with him, the fertile soil and nourishing rain.

> In a dream of the god El, the kindly and benign,
> In a vision of the creator of creatures,
> From the heavens rains fat,
> The wadis flow with honey.
> The god El, the kindly and benign, is glad.

Baalbek, in present-day Lebanon, is the scene of the ruins of a great ancient city devoted to the worship of Baal. Part of the temple ruins are shown here.

> He sets his feet on the footstool,
> Opens his mouth and laughs;
> He lifts up his voice and cries:
>
> "Now will I sit and rest,
> My soul will have peace in my breast;
> For mighty Baal is alive,
> The Prince, the lord of earth still exists!"

This Canaanite myth is a clear example of the prevailing method of explaining the movements of nature in terms of gods. The changes of the seasons are explained by the death and resurrection of a god. The theme of the dying god was one of the permanent legacies of the Near East; a similar theme is also present in some modern religions.

Israel and a Cultural Revolution

During this same period, the end of the second millennium, a small group of Semitic people migrated from Mesopotamia into the land of Canaan. These people were called Hebrews, and they were shepherds, living off the animals which they tended. Pastoral people are usually on the move in search of water and good grazing land. Very often, they settle down and take up farming. The Hebrews were one such people. One of their leaders, Abraham, left Babylonia with his family to find new land. Some of the Hebrews were captured by the Egyptians and lived for many years as slaves in Egypt. Upon their escape, they moved into Canaan to settle.

In Chapter Two, it was pointed out that friction often develops between pastoral and agricultural people. Herders of animals usually attempt to take rich land from the tillers of the soil. This kind of struggle can be seen in the history of the American West, where cattlemen frequently came to blows with homesteaders. Things were no different in the ancient Near East, and the Hebrews took land from the Canaanites.

The Hebrew Advance. The Hebrews were less civilized and more warlike than the people of Canaan. Their social and political organization was based on the family. The heads of important families, men called *patriarchs,* became leaders of groups of families called *tribes.* There were twelve such Hebrew tribes, and they moved one by one into the fertile land of Palestine. Once there, they added farming to their way of life and began to develop new forms of government.

Much of early Hebrew history involved fierce fighting, usually with the people who already occupied the land which the Hebrews wanted. They attacked Canaanite cities and fought the Philistines who had occupied a large area of Palestine. We know a good deal about the history of the Hebrews because they recorded events themselves. These records were eventually put together into one book, the *Bible.* Many portions of the Bible tell of the conquest of Canaan, a struggle which produced such heroes as Joshua, Gideon, Saul and David. The warrior Goliath, who was killed by the young shepherd David, was a Philistine soldier.

Government. During the struggle for control of the land, the Hebrews lacked a central government. The twelve tribes worked together and chose temporary leaders to fight their battles. Once the Canaanite city of Jerusalem was taken, however, the Hebrews settled down to enjoy the fruits of their battles. Around the year 1000 B.C., they chose a king and developed a strong monarchy which firmly united the tribes. For a short period of time, this Hebrew monarchy was the most powerful government in the land of Syria-Palestine. Even today, this area is of great strategic and political importance.

The Hebrews were able to build a strong state because at this time, the large empires were no longer in existence. Egypt had retreated within its borders, the Hittites had been destroyed and the nations of Mesopotamia were weak. King Solomon, who ruled the Hebrews from 973 to 933 B.C., reigned over a wealthy land, built a large temple and was the equal of other nearby rulers. However, unlike other pastoral people who adopted civilized ways, the Hebrews never totally did away with their old ideas. The tribal chieftains always resented the power of the king and the luxury of his court, and in a short time, the monarchy began to crumble. During the next few hundred years, new and powerful states arose, and the Hebrew kingdom was gradually dismembered. In 933 B.C., the kingdom split into two, Israel in the north and Judah in the south. In 586 B.C., Jerusalem itself was captured by the Babylonians. The temple was destroyed, and the Hebrews once again were carried into slavery. After this time, the Hebrews never again regained their military and political strength, and they ceased to be a major power.

The Hebrews left no monuments in stone as did other civilizations, and their period of political power was insignificant compared with the lengthy imperial rule of other nations. They seem, on the surface, to be just another small group of shepherds who gained power for a short time and then sank into oblivion. Why, then, do we study their civilization? The answer lies in their religious and ethical ideas. These people, who were so insignificant in their own time, developed spiritual ideas which have influenced later civilizations, particularly our own, infinitely more than have the accomplishments of other more imposing ancient peoples. The vision of man, society and the universe which was recorded in the Hebrew Bible lived on long after the pyramids were abandoned and the cities of Sumer were covered by the sands of the desert.

It is true that the Hebrews borrowed from other, older civilizations. They did not invent writing, the alphabet, bronze, iron or the basic rules for group living. Nor did they alone develop religious and ethical beliefs. These things had all been developed before them. But, in their borrowing, they infused ideas with new insights, and they created some totally new concepts. They gathered together prevailing ideas and gave them their own special stamp. Through this process, a revolutionary new vision of society, god and the destiny of mankind came about.

The Hebrews broke loose from the long standing belief in nature religion and polytheism. In their culture, the concept of a single god developed, a god who moved in a way which no other ancient people ever dreamed of. The full implications of this accomplishment cannot be grasped quickly. This is why the last unit of this book is devoted entirely to the ideas of the Hebrews. Here let us look at two fragments from the Bible. What revolutionary shift in values is contained in them?

> O Lord, our Lord, how majestic is thy name
>   in all the earth!
> When I look at thy heavens, the work of
>   thy fingers,
> The moon and the stars which thou
>   hast established;
> What is man that thou art mindful
>   of him,
> And the son of man, that thou doest
>   care for him?
> Yet thou has made him little less
>   than God.
> And does crown him with glory
>   and honor.
> Thou hast given him dominion over the
>   works of thy hands;
> Thou has put all things under his feet.
>   PSALMS 8: 1, 3-6
>
> The Lord makes poor and makes rich;
> He brings low, he also exalts.
> He raises up the poor from the dust;
> He lifts the needy from the ash heap,
> To make them sit with princes
> And inherit a seat of honor.
> For the pillars of the earth are the Lord's,
> And on them he has set the world.
>   I SAMUEL 2: 7-8

Out of many events and people, we have chosen those which had importance for the future. The early Iron Age was a period of reformation; old forms were declining, while new inventions and ideas were in the process of formation. The discovery of iron and of alphabetic communication were of immediate revolutionary importance. The Hebrew vision of the world was destined to shake the world, even though at first it seemed out of step with the normal pattern of nature religion as seen in the Canaanite worship of Baal. The next chapter shows how the forces born during the period of the small nations were used and developed, thereby bringing about the climax of Near Eastern civilization.

Define

Carthage   Israel
Mot   Judah
patriarch

Review and Answer

1. The discovery of iron brought about a revolution similar to the Neolithic Revolution. What were some of the economic, social and political consequences of the use of this new metal?
2. What are the differences between pictographic and alphabetic writing?
3. Show how the Canaanite myth of Baal and Anat can be used as an example of mythological thought as described in Reading I (pages 32-33).
4. What are "colonies," and why are they important in the history of human civilization?
5. What is so significant about the two selections (page 124) from the writings of the Hebrews? Do these ideas represent a "cultural revolution"?

9

The Great Empires

Toward the middle of the first millennium, the Near East changed. Large political units, called empires, absorbed the small nations and served to spread the arts of civilization beyond the Near East. Egypt never regained its former power, but peoples both in and around Mesopotamia displayed political power and cultural energy. The Assyrian empire was a reconstruction of the earlier kingdom of Hammurabi. The Lydian kingdom, far to the west in Asia Minor, was a symbol of the spread of civilization. The Persian empire, which spanned the entire range of Near Eastern civilization, from Greece to India, was the capstone of the ancient civilization of the Near East.

Assyria and the Art of War

During the reign of Hammurabi in Babylonia, some people had moved up the Tigris River and settled in the frontier region called Assyria. The major city of this land was Nineveh. The Assyrians continued the basic forms of Babylonian culture, and from the year 900 B.C. on, they became the strongest nation in Mesopotamia. They used cuneiform for their writing and absolute monarchy for their government; they worshipped the same gods as those of Babylonia. The epic of Gilgamesh remained the major work of literature, and it was from tablets found in an Assyrian library that major portions of this tale were pieced together. The architecture and sculpture of the Assyrians are almost identical to those of Babylonia. Assyrian culture represents an extension of Babylonian civilization.

Weapons and Equipment. The Assyrians have one striking claim to fame. They were able to arm their people with iron weapons and develop the most effective war machine that the world had seen. Not only did the Assyrians train their soldiers well, but they added to the technology of war through the invention of equipment. One such invention was the *siege tower*. Important cities were usually built on high ground with heavy walls around them to make them safe from attack. Before the invention of gunpowder, a well fortified city was free from capture as long as its inhabitants could obtain enough food. To cope with this military problem, the Assyrians constructed high, portable towers which could be rolled up to a city wall. Once close to the wall, a ramp over which the attacking soldiers could advance was let down.

So warlike were these people that "Assyrian" has become a byword for militarism. Perhaps it was because Assyria was for so long on the frontier of the civilized world, bearing the brunt of barbarian pressure, that she developed this militaristic streak. In the history of our own civilization, it was Germany which for centuries was on the eastern edge of European civilization. Germany developed a strong military tradition. Geographic location may have much to do with the development of a nation's character.

The Assyrian Conquerors. The Assyrians began to conquer their weaker neighbors. During the reign of Sargon II (721-705 B.C.), most of the small states of Syria-Palestine were destroyed and absorbed into the Assyrian empire. The victors were harsh rulers. Whereas the Egyptians had usually been content to take tribute from conquered lands, the Assyrians destroyed cities and either slaughtered or enslaved entire nations. During this sweep through Palestine, the Kingdom of Israel was destroyed and its inhabitants scattered. In the year 617 B.C., the Assyrians invaded Egypt, and for the first time in history, the valleys of the Nile and the Tigris and Euphrates rivers were united under one government.

Nineveh became the proud capital of the Near East, and into this city flowed the wealth and manpower of an empire. Assyrian buildings were massive, and their sculpture breathed the spirit of power and arrogance. A standard motif in Assyrian art was the figure of a winged bull with the head of a king, usually made in immense proportions and placed at the entry gate of temples and palaces. Assyrian portrayal of humans was generally formal and rather stiff. Their rendition of animals, however, was vibrant and

From the seventh century B.C. comes this sculpture of King Ashurnasirpal II of Assyria attacking a city. Note the siege tower in the center.

full of life. Wall sculptures of hunting scenes, even when standing in modern museums, breathe a vigor and sense of strength.

The Theory of War. War is a major element of human civilization. Much effort could be spent in trying to discover the origin of war and the reasons for its prevalence in human history. This is especially so today, when man has the power to destroy himself. It may be that because man has lived most of his life on earth as a hunter, the killing instinct comprises a large part of his makeup. Yet animals are hunters, but most of them will not fight to the death with their own kind. With few exceptions among the higher animals, only man kills his fellow creatures in an organized fashion.

Before man created civilization, he did not have the means to sustain organized war; most of his energy was spent in keeping himself alive. Once he had gained a surplus supply of food, an army could be created; men could specialize in the art of killing each other. During ancient times, man's technology was not as efficient as it is today, and so he could not make the most of the land which he had. Therefore, one group of people would attack another in order to gain farmland or mineral deposits. The desire for luxury on the part of kings and nobles led them to conquer other lands because they could not make their own land produce the degree of wealth which they wanted.

This practical, or economic, theory of war makes some sense when applied to the ancient world. We have seen the importance of booty to rulers such as Tutmosis of Egypt. The material grandeur of Assyrian culture was made possible because the Assyrian army took wealth, material and slaves from others as prizes of war. Neither the Egyptians nor Assyrians went to war because they believed that their way of life or their religion was superior to those of others. Their wars were not crusades to spread a given ideal. Some wars, however, *are* caused by faith in an ideal. It has been suggested that wars are possible because men are willing to die for a cause. Wars to spread a religion such as Christianity or Islam, or wars to spread a form of government such as communism or democracy, are examples of conflicts caused by a belief in an ideal. Only man involves himself in this sort of conflict.

Whatever the causes of wars, the Assyrians were successful in organizing this kind of human activity. They built a large empire, but they were unable to produce the necessary political skill to make their rule acceptable to others. In the face of Assyrian brutality, rebellions broke out, and in 612 B.C., the city of Nineveh was destroyed. It was never rebuilt. To the south, the Babylonians rose to power, and new people spilled over from the barbarian reservoir. The Assyrians met a violent end, thereby confirming the Biblical saying, "Those who live by the sword will perish by the sword."

How should we assess the Assyrians? They stand condemned for their brutality, but every nation, our own included, has used war in order to grow. The battering down of city walls and the scattering of people did ultimately lead to the unification of much of the ancient world. The road from Nineveh on the Tigris to Thebes on the Nile speeded up the transportation of men, products and ideas. The fact that a traveler on that road would pass by the rubble of destroyed cities should point up, once again, the fact that for every advance made by man, a price must be paid.

Lydia and Coinage

Moving well into the first millennium, the number of nations in the Near East increases. It would be impossible to discuss them all, and so we must choose those which seem to be more important than others. Out of the great number of people who existed at this time, we have chosen the Lydians mainly because they are responsible for an invention equal in importance to that of iron and the alphabet. Coins were first used in Lydia and then became the major instrument of trade in the ancient world. It is perhaps no accident that the legendary King Midas, whose touch turned everything to gold, is said to have lived near the land of the Lydians.

We have seen how trade developed early in man's history as a way of fulfilling his needs. For example, if one man had more food than he himself could eat, but had no weapons, he traded some of his food for weapons. The weapon-maker, of course, must have wanted the food. The Egyptians were skilled craftsmen making pottery and jewelry, but the land of Egypt has no forests. As a result, Egyptian merchants took their valuable trinkets to Lebanon, a portion of Syria which was heavily forested. The rulers of this land wanted the finery of Egypt and traded their timber for it. This process of exchanging goods is called *barter*. It is an economic activity requiring at least two people, each one wanting what the other has. To accomplish the trade, some rules of exchange would have to be agreed on, for example, so many necklaces would be worth so many logs. Also, the goods themselves would have to be carried to a meeting place and exchanged on the spot. If one person, or nation, did not have what the other wanted, no trade could take place.

The Development of a Medium of Exchange. Under these kinds of conditions, trade was rather limited. However, the desire of man to fulfill his needs led him to make some inventions designed to increase the scope of trade. If everyone could agree on some material which could serve as a symbol for a fixed amount of wealth, a person could exchange his timber for a certain amount of this material. He could then take this material, this symbol of wealth, to another person and give it to him in exchange for another product. The material served as a *medium of exchange*. It helped to increase trade because a merchant no longer had to carry with him exactly what another person might want. He could sell his product for some of the "medium of exchange" and then buy what he wanted with this same medium.

Of course, men would have to agree upon an actual material to use as the medium of exchange. Gold was chosen for this purpose. Gold is a bright, attractive metal, in limited supply, which is not strong enough to use for either tools or weapons. It also does not rust or decay as do other metals. Gold became, and remains today, the symbol of wealth, at times still serving as a medium of exchange. People who possessed gold could obtain products without having other products with which to trade. The desire to acquire gold became a powerful motive in human affairs.

The Kingdom of Lydia was located on the western border of the Near East in the western part of Asia Minor just across the Aegean Sea from Greece. This area was never conquered by the Assyrians, and a wealthy kingdom grew up there. One of the kings of Lydia was Croesus (CREE suhs), a wealthy ruler who possessed vast quantities of gold. The expression "as rich as Croesus" is used even today to describe a very wealthy person.

The Invention of Coins. It was in Lydia that the idea was born to make small circular pieces of metal called coins. One small coin could be worth many pounds of gold if everyone was willing to accept the coin rather than the gold. It must have taken a long time for merchants to accept a small piece of metal as being worth several bars of gold. However, the efficiency of the idea made its acceptance inevitable. It was now no longer necessary for merchants to travel about with bulky bars of gold in their ships. With coins, the volume of trade could increase tremendously, for merchants could travel with vast amounts of wealth in their pockets.

Because of this invention, wealth—and the power it brought—could be spread great distances with relative ease. The economic basis of civilization became attainable in lands which before had been unable to move beyond the Neolithic level. We can say that perhaps a trio of inventions—iron, the alphabet and coinage—all made possible the spread and elaboration of civilization. Man now had the power to expand more rapidly and with greater force than ever before.

Persia and Its Empire

The Assyrian empire, which had fallen so rapidly in the seventh century, had received its blows not only from subjected peoples but from fresh waves of invaders from the north and east. To the east of Mesopotamia lies the land of Iran, which served as a reservoir of pastoral people, mostly Indo-European in background. After the collapse of the Assyrian empire, new people moved into the civilized area of the Near East. One new group of people were the Greeks, who at this time had little influence on the Near East. One of the Greek immigrants was a historian by the name of Herodotus (hih RAHD uh tuhs), who recorded many events which took place in the Near East. His book is one of our best sources for the history of this period, and it is from Herodotus that we learn of the defeat of Lydia's King Croesus at the hands of a new people, the Persians.

The Persians were Indo-Europeans who moved into the civilized area from the plains of Iran, bringing with them vigorous leadership and new ideas. Within a short period of time, they had become the rulers of the entire Near East. In fact, this feat was begun and almost totally accomplished during the reign of one Persian king, Cyrus, founder of the Achaemenid (uh KEE muh nihd) dynasty, who ruled from 550 to 539 B.C. The fact that a military and political accomplishment which had been the dream of rulers for centuries could be accomplished in this short time shows to what extent the tempo of man's history had changed since the days of the Sumerian city-states.

Cyrus and the Persian Conquest. The story of the man, Cyrus, and of his people, the Persians, is told by Herodotus in a way which no other historian can hope to equal. The Persians began as simple folk living on the outskirts of civilization, and Cyrus began from humble origins to forge the Persians into a powerful nation. No doubt there had been other leaders as heroic as Cyrus, but until this time, the world had not seen one man become the builder of a nation and of an empire during his own lifetime.

When Cyrus was about to be born, it was predicted that he would rule all of Asia. Jealous noblemen gave the baby to a cowherd to be put to death, but the cowherd took pity on the child and raised him as his own son. The boy's kingly powers were revealed in an incident recorded by Herodotus.

> When the boy was in his tenth year, an accident which I will now relate caused it to be discovered who he was. He was at play one day in the village where the folds of the cattle were, along with other boys of his own age, in the street. The other boys who were playing with him chose the cowherd's son, as he was called, to be their king. He then proceeded to order them about—some he set to build him houses, others he made his guards, one of them was to be the king's eye, another had the office of carrying his messages, all had some task or other. Among the boys there was one . . . who refused to do what Cyrus had set him. Cyrus told the other boys to take him into custody, and when his orders were obeyed, he chastised him most severely with the whip.

It seems that this boy was the son of a nobleman, and when his father complained, Cyrus showed the strength and nobility of his own character when he answered:

> I treated him as he deserved. I was chosen king in play by the boys of our village, because they thought me the best for it. He himself was one of the boys who chose me. All the others did according to my orders; but he refused, and made light of them, until at last he got his due reward. If for this I deserve to suffer punishment, here I am ready to submit to it.

THE GREAT EMPIRES   133

The instincts for leadership which Cyrus displayed as a child enabled him to become king of the Persians. Upon becoming king, he first led the Persians to the east, giving them control over all the lands up to the borders of India. He then pushed west, crossing and conquering the land once ruled by the Assyrians. When he came to Sardis, the capital of Lydia, his rude warriors were in marked contrast to the wealth and power of the Lydian army. Herodotus tells how Cyrus used what resources he had against a superior force.

> When Cyrus beheld the Lydians arranging themselves in order of battle . . . [and] fearful of the strength of their cavalry, he adopted a device. . . . He collected together all the camels that had come in the train of his army to carry the provisions and the baggage, and taking off their loads, he mounted riders upon them accoutred as horsemen. These he commanded to advance in front of his other troops against the Lydian horses; behind them were to follow the foot soldiers, and last of all the cavalry. When his

One of the best examples of Assyrian sculpture is this wounded lioness, dating from the sixth century B.C. The sculptor's skill in portraying the power and strength of the dying animal is clearly evident.

British Museum

arrangements were complete, he gave his troops orders to slay all the other Lydians who came in their way without mercy, but to spare Croesus and not kill him, even if he should be seized and offer resistance. The reason why Cyrus opposed his camels to the enemy's horses was because the horse has a natural dread of the camel, and cannot abide either the sight or the smell of that animal. By this stratagem he hoped to make Croesus's horses useless to him, the horse being what he chiefly depended on for victory. The two armies then joined battle, and immediately the Lydian war-horses, seeing and smelling the camels, turned round and galloped off; and it came to pass that all Croesus's hopes withered away.

From Lydia, Cyrus moved to the heartland of civilization itself, and in 539 B.C., entered through the gates of Babylon. The mighty city surrendered quickly. Cyrus was killed while trying to subdue the barbarian tribes in the north, but his son finished the job by conquering Egypt. Destiny seemed to be with the Persians; they were the wave of the future. Never before had events moved so rapidly and on so wide a scale.

The Persian Empire. Unlike the Assyrians, the Persians were able to build a stable empire. They did not loot cities and enslave people but rather left their subjects generally alone to manage their local affairs in their own manner. Taxes were levied and men drafted to fill the army, but on the whole, the Persians were not harsh rulers. They seemed to have a genius for imperial rule. In each province of the empire, a Persian governor, called a *satrap* (SAY trap), was placed in command. He was responsible for the rule of his province, but he usually respected the people's religion and customs. The Persians created unity but retained freedom and diversity. For example, they permitted the Hebrews to leave Babylon and return to Palestine to practice their own religion.

The Persians put into practice the advice which was given by Croesus to Cyrus after the capture of Sardis. Once again, Herodotus is our source of information.

> After a while, happening to turn and perceive the Persian soldiers engaged in plundering the town, [Croesus] said to Cyrus, "May I now tell you, O King, what I have in my mind, or is silence best?" Cyrus bade him speak his mind boldly. Then he put this question. "What is it, Cyrus, which those men yonder are doing so busily?" "Plundering your city," Cyrus answered, "and carrying off your riches." "Not my city," rejoined the other, "nor my riches. They are not mine any more. It is your wealth which they are pillaging."

Unlike the Egyptians, the Persians did not regard the empire as a collection of wealth to be carried off to the home country. Persia did not fasten itself like a parasite on the Near East. It became the Near East.

The King's Highway, which stretched from the capital city of Susa in the east to the city of Sardis in the west, was a fitting symbol of Persian government. This road was used to transport troops, but it also served to speed up the movement of products, ideas and people. It helped to break down local prejudices and brought about a sense of unity. This royal road did for the Near East what the transcontinental railroads did for the United States. They both bound different groups of people together into one nation. Herodotus traveled the King's Highway and recorded the motto of the Persian royal messengers—"Neither snow, nor rain, nor heat, nor gloom of night stays these couriers from the swift completion of their appointed rounds." Perhaps it is no accident that the United States Post Office chose this very motto as its own.

Explaining the Persian Successes. What reason or reasons can we give for the rapid success of the Persians? Were they superhuman? Were the civilizations of the Nile and Euphrates so old and worn out that they would have collapsed before the invasion of any new people? Or was the Persian empire created by one man, Cyrus, whose personal strength and intelligence made the difference? These are not idle questions, and the way we answer them depends on our own philosophy of life. Some people look at human events and see individual great men shaping these events. Other people look at the same events and see circumstances and long-range trends as the more important factors. Any one event can be interpreted many ways. Looking at the rapid growth of the Persian empire, a few comments can be made.

It is true that as a society becomes increasingly civilized, it becomes more complex. Wealth is not equally distributed, and many different classes develop. Very often, friction, and sometimes civil war, occur. A less developed society, like that of the Persians in their early days, is free of these tensions and has a high degree of unity. When the Persians moved down the valley of the Tigris-Euphrates, Babylon was suffering from internal discord. This fact might help explain why the Persians captured this city with ease.

By the time the Persians reached the Nile, the existing Egyptian civilization was very old and had changed very little since the early days. Because the Egyptians had had an almost unbroken

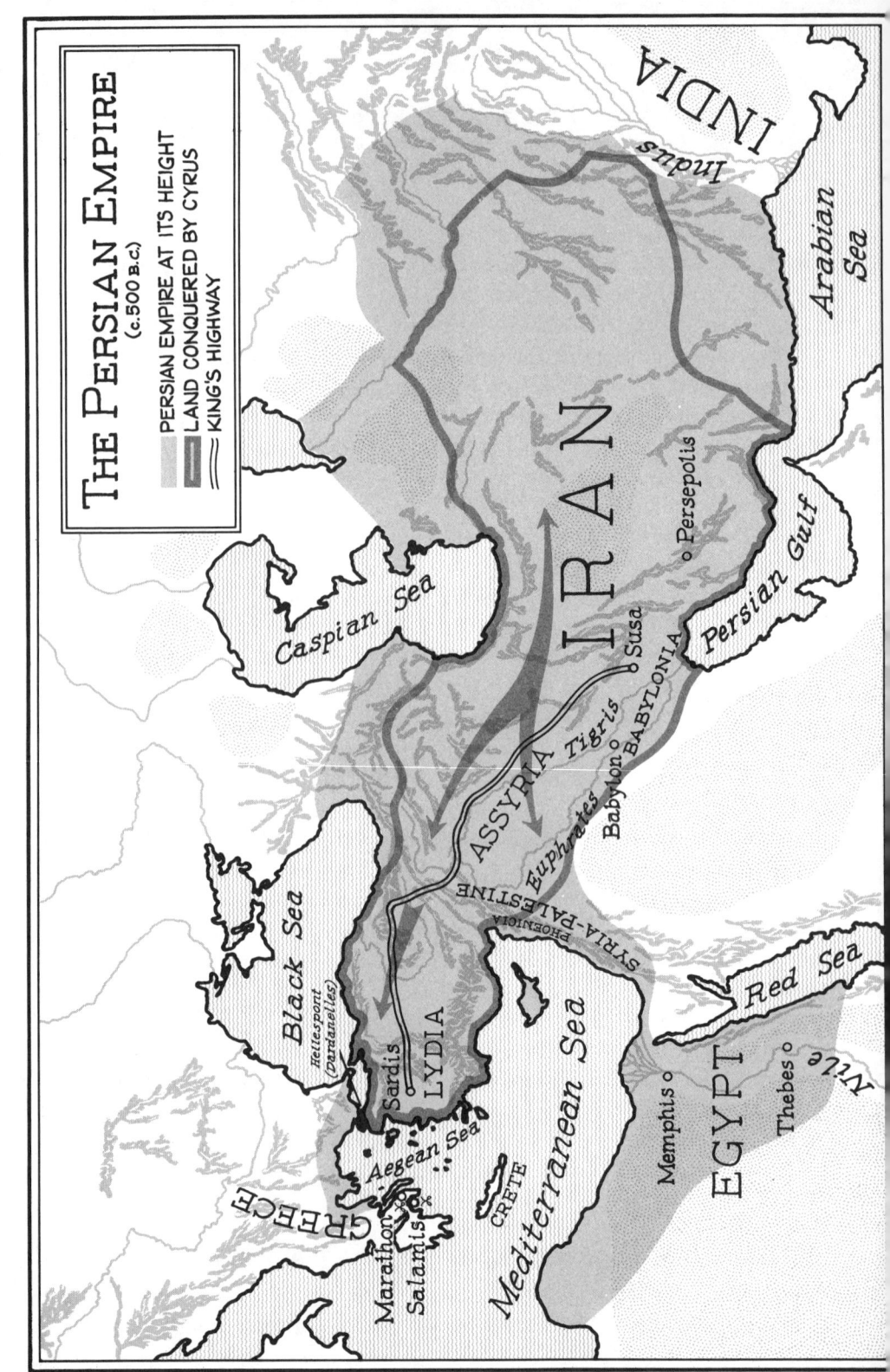

history stretching back thousands of years, their way of life was, in a sense, frozen, and they were incapable of generating new ideas. We have seen how even a pharaoh was unable to reform Egyptian religion. In spite of their many accomplishments, the Egyptians were unable to change to meet new conditions, and they fell under the Persian onslaught.

From these two examples, we might conclude that circumstances did seem to favor a new people like the Persians. But can we overlook the individual man who galvanized the Persians into action and led them to victory? Without Cyrus, could the Persians have unified the Near East even if conditions did seem to favor them? Here the historian can give no final answer, for unlike science, history follows no fixed laws. The emergence of a great individual, a Cyrus, Caesar, Napoleon or Lincoln cannot be predicted, and such a person can reverse trends and overcome circumstances. About all that can be said at this point is that in human events, the man and the times must converge. Individuals make history, but circumstances influence their actions.

Religious Ideas. The Persians produced influential ideas in fields other than war and politics. On the plains of Iran, the homeland of the Persians, a new religion was formed. The Persians, like most of the other Near Eastern peoples, practiced a form of nature religion with appropriate gods and myths. However, as the Persians were conquering the Near East, a religion which did away with many accepted ideas was conquering the Persians. The ideas which clustered around this religious movement were developed by a thinker named Zoroaster, and the religion itself is called *Zoroastrianism.*

Zoroaster was a religious reformer who preached a strict moral and ethical code and the worship of a god of light and wisdom. This god was *Ahura Mazda* (AH hoo ruh MAHZ duh), meaning "wise lord," and he was the force and intelligence which created and ruled the universe. Zoroaster had little use for elaborate ceremonies and sacrifices. The only ritual connected with his religion seems to have been the tending of a sacred fire, symbol of the god of light. Zoroastrianism became, for a while, the official religion of

As the map on the opposite page shows, the Persians had built a huge empire by 500 B.C. Their threat to Greece and beyond was ended by small determined forces of Greeks at Marathon and Salamis.

the Persian empire, and it represents a new spirit in man's religious quest. Consider the following extract from the *Avesta*, the sacred book of Zoroastrianism.

> I question thee, Lord: Answer me.
> Who was at its birth the first father of Justice?
> Who assigned their paths to sun and stars?
> Who was it, if not thou, that makes the moon wax and wane?
> That is what I wish to know, Wise One, and other things too.
> Who established heaven and earth so that they fall not?
> Who brought forth the waters and the plants?
> Who harnessed the horses to the winds and the clouds?
> What craftsman made light and darkness?
> What craftsman made sleep and wakefulness?
> Who created morning, noon and evening
> To mark his task for him who understands. . . ?
>
> I question thee Lord: Answer me.
>
> Who formed Devotion, consecrated in Rule?
> Who made the son respectful to his father?
> I try so to understand thee, Wise One,
> As a holy spirit creator of all things.

Clearly this is a story of creation, told in the form of questions. Compare the style and spirit of this account with the Babylonian myth of creation. How different is that account from the Persian one? What seems significant is the fact that Ahura Mazda, the "Wise One," is not involved in the natural process as are other gods. He does not seem to be a divine person but rather divine wisdom or intelligence. He is called a "craftsman" and seems to have created the universe from above rather than from within. Even the form of the story, a series of searching questions, seems to indicate an emphasis placed on the mind and reason.

Persian Monotheism. Zoroastrianism is a kind of monotheism. The rampant polytheism which can be seen so clearly in other myths is lacking here. Both Persian and Hebrew monotheism grew up at about the same time. To what extent one influenced the other is difficult to say, but their coming seemed to signify the beginning of a shift of values, a new force at work in the minds of men. Zoroastrianism was not a pure monotheism, for there was also a god of darkness who did battle with Ahura Mazda for control of the world and of individual men. The existence of two gods served to explain the existence of evil in the world; evil was the work of the god of darkness. This concept of religious dualism did not exist among the Hebrews, but it was to have an influence long after the Persians were gone.

The Oriental Institute, The University of Chicago

Evidence of the massive nature of Persian architecture and sculpture is the Palace of Darius with the Great Stairway with Ten Thousand Immortals in the foreground. The palace, located at the ancient site of Persepolis in present-day Iran, was built between 521 and 465 B.C.

Zoroastrianism survived the eventual disintegration of the Persian empire and has some followers even today. However, it is not a major world religion. Other forms of faith proved more attractive to the Persians, and the religion of Zoroaster is mainly of historical interest. Nonetheless, it provided some new values. It placed a strong emphasis on ethical living, and it drew man's attention away from elaborate nature mythology and complicated rituals. Perhaps it served to give the Persians the moral strength needed to rule an empire successfully. The Greeks said that a young Persian was taught three things: to ride a horse, to shoot an arrow and to speak only the truth. This was high praise coming from enemies of the Persians.

Later Persian Rulers. Cyrus' son Cambyses (kam BI seez), who ruled from 530 to 521 B.C., conquered Egypt, thereby unifying, at least in a political sense, the entire Near East. Following Cambyses was Darius (duh RI uhs), who reigned until 486 B.C. Darius absorbed into the empire the Greek settlers on the coast of Asia Minor. He then moved the Persians on to the sea in an attempt to invade and conquer Greece itself. Surprisingly enough, he was defeated by the Greeks at the small village of Marathon and was forced to turn back. The Battle of Marathon (490 B.C.) was a crucial battle in the history of Europe. To grasp its full significance, we must first study the Greeks themselves, a subject for another book.

Darius was followed by King Xerxes (ZURK seez), whose reign lasted until 465 B.C.; Xerxes presided over the Persian empire at the time of its greatest extent. In order to avenge the defeat of Darius, Xerxes crossed the Hellespont, the narrow strip of water which separates Europe from Asia. He wanted to unite Europe and Asia as his forebears had united Egypt and Mesopotamia. Perched on his throne overlooking the Bay of Salamis near Athens, Xerxes saw his fleet destroyed by the Greeks. He was forced to retreat, and Persia was destined to remain a Near Eastern power.

In spite of these setbacks on the fringes of the empire, Xerxes could well call himself "King of Kings," for he ruled over many of the ancient nations. After the reign of Xerxes, the empire ran into difficulties. Eventually, the Greeks took the offensive, and during the next century (the fourth century B.C.), they conquered Persia and spread their culture throughout the Near East. With the Persians, the history of the ancient Near East came to an end.

This unit has covered about seven centuries—1200 to 500 B.C. We have seen the arts of civilization developed by an increasing number of people, and we have seen the area of civilization spread by means of new inventions and discoveries. Which of these ideas, people or inventions is the most important? Each person must answer that question for himself. In this unit, we have also looked into the ideas developed by a relatively insignificant people, the Hebrews. The next unit will be devoted entirely to them.

Define

Nineveh
barter
medium of exchange
Croesus

Herodotus
Cyrus
satrap
Zoroastrianism

Ahura Mazda
Darius
Xerxes

Review and Answer

1. What are the Assyrians remembered for? Is it significant that they could portray animals better than humans in their art?

THE GREAT EMPIRES   141

2. What is the economic theory of the origin of war? What is an ideological war?
3. Explain the various ways in which trade can be carried on.
4. How did the Persian empire differ from other empires?
5. Why was the King's Highway an important symbol in human history?
6. Why was Xerxes called the "King of Kings"?

The pyramids of Egypt stand today, bearing witness through the ages that a powerful civilization once existed in ancient times. We have always known of ancient Egypt, but other civilizations were unknown until recent years when archaeologists began to dig them up. There is one other ancient people who have been better known than even the Egyptians. Generations of people in the Western world have known of the Hebrews. For many individuals, the landscape of ancient Israel is more familiar to them than is the landscape of their neighboring county. The Hebrews did not have to be archaeologically discovered for the simple reason that the Bible, a record of their history and culture, is one of the best known works of literature in our civilization.

The Old Testament, that portion of the Bible which deals with the Hebrews, is not a single book. It is a collection of different books, each having been written at a different time. The books of the Bible were written usually long after the events which they describe, and they were gathered together very late in the history of Israel. Some portions of the Bible are stories, some are historical accounts, others are poems and proverbs, and some contain the words of religious thinkers. As is true of all collections, some sections of the Bible are more significant than others, but most of it is the major source of our knowledge of the Hebrew civilization. Segments of the Bible will appear in this unit; other, more extensive selections are in the Readings.

UNIT V
The Revolution Within Civilization: Israel

10

The Development of Monotheism

Since the Bible is the Hebrews' own account of their history, its reliability might be questioned. However, in recent years, archaeologists working in Palestine have discovered concrete evidence confirming most of the historical accuracy of the Bible. As we have seen, the actual history of the Hebrews was not remarkable. They migrated to Canaan, established a short-lived monarchy and were defeated and reduced to the role of a minor power. What *is* important about their history is the way they themselves viewed it and the concept they had of their own destiny. The ideas which they developed while describing themselves have had as great an impact upon the development of civilization as the accomplishments of all other Near Eastern peoples put together. The Hebrews brought about a spiritual revolution.

The Separation of Religion from Nature

Religion in the Near East focused on nature. For most people, the divine forces of nature, conceived in the form of gods, were identified with the forces of nature. The Sumerian god Enlil was the air and storm. The Babylonian goddess Ishtar was the planet Venus. Tiamat was the substance out of which the universe was fashioned. Even Aton, the god worshipped by the pharaoh Akhnaton, was the sun. The gods were intertwined with nature.

For some unknown reason, the Hebrews possessed the insight to conceive of the divine force as being outside of nature. They separated religion from nature and affirmed the belief in a god who transcended nature. This god they called *Yahweh*.* Yahweh created man and the universe, but he did all of this from an exalted position. Nature was his handiwork, "the work of his fingers," and he controlled its actions, but he was not a part of the natural process.

This concept of a transcendent god is of the greatest importance. It is the source of Hebrew creativity, and it is the basic assumption underlying the modern notion of God. Because of this belief, the natural environment of man was totally his to move about in. Nature was no longer sacred in the way that it once had been; it was no longer mythological. For this reason, the Hebrew beliefs are not nature myths; they serve a different function as we will soon see. This revolution in values allowed religious thought to move into different areas of action. For example, the practice of magic was never tolerated among the Hebrews. The secrets of the universe were not to be discovered by using nature in this mechanical way.

The process of removing the divine force from nature took a long time. Since the Bible was written at a time when Hebrew ideas had already been developed, it is difficult for us to observe this process. In the Bible, there are only hints which show the actual development of a transcendent god. When Yahweh spoke to Moses, he spoke through a burning bush, a fact which would indicate that God was still tied up with nature. When the prophet Amos speaks of the Lord roaring from Zion, he could mean that the voice of God is heard through the thunder. However, consider the following way in which Yahweh appeared to Elijah.

> And behold, the Lord passed by, and a great and strong wind rent the mountains, and broke in pieces the rocks before the Lord, but the Lord was not in the wind; and after the wind an earthquake, but the Lord was not in the earthquake; and after the earthquake a fire, but the Lord was not in the fire; and after the fire a still, small voice. And when Elijah heard it, he wrapped his face in his mantle and went out and stood at the entrance of the

---

* It is difficult to use the exact name of the Hebrew god. The Hebrew name for their god is YHWH, but to them, the concept of god was so holy that his name could not be pronounced. Therefore, they took the vowels from another word which meant "lord" and added them to the four sacred consonants. The result was Yahweh, and this is the term for God used in this chapter. It is the closest to the Hebrew usage. Selections from the Bible quoted in this chapter are taken from the Revised Standard Version which uses the words "Lord" or "God," following the Latin usage of *Dominus* and *Deus*.

cave. And behold, there came a voice to him and said, "What are you doing here, Elijah?"

I KINGS 19: 11-13

The powerful forces of nature, wind, earthquake and fire do not contain God. Rather, he comes in a "still, small voice." The Bible does not say specifically where this voice comes from. Perhaps it comes from within Elijah; it seems to speak directly to his mind and heart. God can no longer be easily located; nature is no longer the dwelling place of the divine.

The Covenant and Monotheism

The best known accomplishment of the Hebrew civilization was the development of the concept of one God—*monotheism*. The urge to discover a sense of oneness in the universe had been felt by many people. Akhnaton, when faced with the multitude of Egyptian gods, tried without success to establish one god who would offer unity to Egyptian religion. Zoroaster worshipped one god, the divine intelligence which created the world and gave insight and wisdom to men. However, Zoroastrianism failed to retain a hold on the Persians once they had occupied the entire Near East. The old gods of Egypt and Mesopotamia eventually triumphed.

The Swing from Polytheism to Monotheism. Cyrus accepted Marduk of Babylon as a valid god and claimed that Marduk favored him rather than the Babylonians. Polytheism was, to many ancient peoples, a more logical form of religion than monotheism. The world consists of different people, why not different gods? Since nature was so varied, each natural force was in itself a different god. True monotheism can only come about when nature is separated from religion, and it was the Hebrews who paved the way for a belief in one God.

Some historians believe that prehistoric man had conceived of a single divine force permeating the universe—a kind of primitive monotheism. According to their theory, as man became civilized and developed the scope of his thinking, his religion became more complex. Polytheism and an elaborate mythology seem to have been natural results of civilization.

As we have seen, the myths surrounding the Sumerian and Babylonian gods gave them each a strong and distinct personality. It was almost impossible for these gods to give way to a single god.

THE DEVELOPMENT OF MONOTHEISM 147

They were strong deities identified with powerful forces of nature. A kind of vague "super-god," or overall divine force, was difficult to conceive of and to make acceptable to many people. Akhnaton's god, for example, was too abstract and distant to catch the imagination of people accustomed to living among the colorful gods of popular mythology. Why then were the Hebrews able to develop an unbreakable faith in a single god?

There is no clear-cut answer to this question. Only a few attempts at an explanation can be made. When the Hebrews moved into Canaan and adopted civilized ways, they were a simple, pastoral people. They were newcomers in a strange land, and some of them had once been enslaved by the Egyptians. Their greatest source of strength was a faith in a tribal god, a father-figure who promised to give them a land of their own if they would serve him. This God, whom the Hebrews called Yahweh, demanded strict obedience and exclusive worship.

The demands of Yahweh were embodied in a set of ten commandments which were given to the leader Moses on a mountaintop. The first of these commandments read, "Thou shalt have no other gods before me." Yahweh was a jealous God who required devoted worship. This challenge of Yahweh was met by a succession of leaders who used persuasion and force to keep their people from worshipping other gods, gods who appeared so much more natural and easygoing. When Moses returned from Mt. Sinai with the commandments from Yahweh, he found his people worshipping a golden calf, the symbol of worldly prosperity and abundance.

> And as soon as he came near the camp and saw the calf and the dancing, Moses' anger burned hot, and he threw the tables out of his hands and broke them at the foot of the mountain. And he took the calf which they had made, and burnt it with fire, and ground it to powder, and scattered it upon the water, and made the people of Israel drink it.
>
> EXODUS 32: 19-20

It was vigorous leaders like Moses who made the Hebrews willing to accept the hard and poor life which they experienced in the wilderness before they entered the land of Canaan.

Yahweh and the Covenant. The agreement made between the Hebrews and Yahweh was called the *covenant*. It served as the basic element in the structure of their religion. This concept of the covenant can be seen throughout Hebrew history, appearing in different forms and on various levels. The covenant with Yahweh gave the early leaders of Israel the physical courage to face people

Alinari—Art Reference Bureau

Unlike later generations of non-Hebrew artists and sculptors, the ancient Hebrews themselves produced very little art. However, outstanding Hebrew figures from the Old Testament provided the inspiration for many artists. This statue of Moses was created by the Italian sculptor Michaelangelo in the early 1500's A.D.

much stronger than they in terms of military power. When the shepherd boy David approached the strapping Philistine warrior Goliath, David was armed with only a slingshot, but Goliath had the best equipment of war. But David believed that he was armed with something more, and he said to his opponent:

> You come to me with a sword and with a spear and with a javelin; but I come to you in the name of the Lord of hosts, the God of the armies of Israel, whom you have defied. This day the Lord will deliver you into my hand, and I will strike you down and cut off your head; and I will give the dead bodies of the host of the Philistines this day to the birds of the air and to the wild beasts of the earth; that all the earth may know that there is a God in Israel, and that all this assembly may know that the Lord saves not with the sword and spear; for the battle is the Lord's, and he will give you into our hand.
>
> I Samuel 17: 45-47

This is an interesting account, for it shows the disdain which David had for the symbols of worldly power, as well as the faith which the Hebrews had in their covenant with Yahweh. The story indicates something else about the Hebrews. Their account of the battle shows that David was aided by a supernatural power, but it also shows that he killed Goliath in a naturalistic manner. Goliath's temples were exposed, and David hit him with a stone at this one open spot. While unconscious from this blow, his head was severed from his body. David performed an apparently impossible feat, and his victory confirmed the Hebrews' faith in Yahweh. However, this victory was not brought about by magical devices.

The Hebrew Faith. Victories on the field of battle gave substance to the promise of Yahweh. But the covenant moved on a deeper level of faith as can be seen in the case of Abraham, the man called by Yahweh to leave his home in Mesopotamia to establish a new nation.

> The Lord said to Abraham . . . "Lift up your eyes, and look from the place where you are, northward and southward and eastward and westward; for all the land which you see I will give to you and to your descendants for ever. I will make your descendants as the dust of the earth; so that if one can count the dust of the earth your descendants also can be counted."
>
> GENESIS 13: 14-16

Armed with this promise, Abraham set out, but troubles beset him. He and his wife Sarah had no children, and Sarah was well beyond the age of childbearing. How would the promised descendants be born? Then, in her old age, Sarah gave birth to a son named Isaac; the hope for the future rested with him. At this point, there occurs in the Bible an episode which, in the simplest of language, lays bare the depth of the faith which the covenant produced.

> After these things God tested Abraham, and said to him, "Abraham!" And he said, "Here am I." He said, "Take your son, your only son Isaac, whom you love, and go to the land of Moriah, and offer him there as a burnt offering upon one of the mountains of which I shall tell you." So Abraham rose early in the morning, saddled his ass, and took two of his young men with him, and his son Isaac; and he cut the wood for the burnt offering, and arose and went to the place of which God had told him. On the third day Abraham lifted up his eyes and saw the place afar off. Then Abraham said to his young men, "Stay here with the ass; I and the lad will go yonder and worship, and come again to you." And Abraham took the wood of the burnt offering, and laid it on Isaac his son; and he took in his hand the fire and the knife. So they went both of them together. And Isaac said to his father Abraham, "My father!" And he said, "Here am I, my son." He said, "Behold, the fire and the wood; but where is the lamb for a burnt offering?" Abraham said, "God will provide himself the lamb for a burnt offering, my son." So they went both of them together.
>
> When they came to the place of which God had told him, Abraham built an altar there, and laid the wood in order, and bound Isaac his son, and laid him on the altar, upon the wood. Then Abraham put forth his hand, and took the knife to slay his son. But the angel of the Lord called to him from heaven, and said, "Abraham, Abraham!" And he said, "Here am I." He said,

"Do not lay your hand on the lad or do anything to him; for now I know that you fear God, seeing you have not withheld your son, your only son, from me." And Abraham lifted up his eyes and looked, and behold, behind him was a ram, caught in a thicket by his horns; and Abraham went and took the ram, and offered it up as a burnt offering instead of his son. . . .

And the angel of the Lord called to Abraham a second time from heaven, and said "By myself I have sworn, says the Lord, because you have done this, and have not withheld your son, your only son, I will indeed bless you, and I will multiply your descendants as the stars of heaven and as the sand which is on the seashore. And your descendants shall possess the gate of their enemies, and by your descendants shall all of the nations of the earth bless themselves, because you have obeyed my voice." So Abraham returned to his young men, and they arose and went together to Beersheba, and Abraham dwelt at Beersheba.

GENESIS 22: 1-19

Abraham had more to do than face a warrior on the battlefield. He was willing to give up everything, not only his son but the hope of the future. By human standards, Yahweh's command was illogical, for he had promised to Abraham powerful descendants. How would they come about if Isaac were killed? But the Hebrews believed that Yahweh was not bound by the limits of human reason, and by being willing to give up all that he had lived for, Abraham secured for Israel the hope of an even greater future. "By your descendants shall all the nations of the earth bless themselves, because you have obeyed my voice."

Perhaps because of this faith in their future, the Hebrews showed little mercy toward those who stood in the way of them and of their destiny. The Egyptians who pursued the escaping Hebrews were drowned in the sea; the people of Israel rejoiced, saying, "The Lord is a man of war. Sing to the Lord for he has triumphed gloriously; the horse and his rider he has thrown into the sea." The inhabitants of Canaan were conquered, and their cities occupied. Yahweh led the Hebrew generals, at times giving them advice about military strategy. The city of Jericho was captured in a remarkable manner. The Sixth Chapter of the Book of Joshua in the Old Testament describes this attack. The entire Book of Judges, beginning with Chapter Two, provides an exciting account of the vigorous and often bloody way in which the early Hebrews moved into the land of Palestine.

While the Hebrews were fighting to gain control of the fertile land in Palestine, faith in Yahweh remained strong. But once the

Hebrews had settled down, taken up farming and attained wealth and political power, other gods became increasingly attractive. This development was only natural, for the nature gods of Canaan had been worshipped for centuries, and they represented a logical kind of religion for a settled people. Many of the Hebrews worshipped Baal as well as Yahweh. Even King Solomon, the most powerful of the Hebrew monarchs, tolerated the worship of many different gods. The covenant was being broken.

The Prophets: Monotheism and Ethical Values

The worship of Yahweh might have disappeared had not a group of religious leaders appeared who kept the Hebrews true to their earlier faith. These leaders were called *prophets*. Yahweh's prophets were men drawn from all classes of society, and they claimed to speak the true commandments and desires of Yahweh. They did not use magic to predict the future, but they often had the insight to see the consequences of men's actions. They openly criticized established religious leaders, and often, the kings themselves. It was these prophets who kept the faith in Yahweh alive, and it was they who fashioned the concepts and ideas which have given Hebrew thought its great power and influence.

Elijah. The prophets of Yahweh cried out against the worship of other gods. The Bible tells of a dramatic encounter between the prophet Elijah and the prophets of Baal.

> And Elijah came near to all the people, and said, "How long will you go limping with two different opinions? If the Lord is God, follow him; but if Baal, then follow him." And the people did not answer him a word. Then Elijah said to the people, "I, even I only, am left a prophet of the Lord; but Baal's prophets are four hundred and fifty men. Let two bulls be given to us; and let them choose one bull for themselves, and cut it in pieces and lay it on the wood, but put no fire to it; and I will prepare the other bull and lay it on the wood, and put no fire to it. And you call on the name of your god and I will call on the name of the Lord; and the God who answers by fire, he is God." And all the people answered, "It is well spoken."
>
> And they took the bull which was given them, and they prepared it, and called on the name of Baal from morning until noon, saying, "O Baal, answer us!" But there was no voice and no one answered. And they limped about the altar which they had made. And at noon Elijah mocked them, saying, "Cry aloud, for he is a god; either he is musing, or he has gone aside, or he is

on a journey, or perhaps he is asleep and must be awakened." And they cried aloud, and cut themselves after their custom with swords and lances, until the blood gushed out upon them. And as midday passed, they raved on until the time of the offering of the oblation, but there was no voice; no one answered, no one heeded.

And at the time of the offering of the oblation, Elijah the prophet came near and said, "O Lord, God of Abraham, Isaac, and Israel, let it be known this day that thou art God in Israel, and that I am thy servant, that I have done all these things at thy word. Answer me, O Lord, answer me, that this people may know that thou, O Lord, art God, and that thou has turned their hearts back." Then the fire of the Lord fell, and consumed the burnt offering and the word, and the stones, and the dust, and licked up the water that was in the trench. And when all the people saw it, they fell on their faces; and they said, "The Lord, he is God; the Lord, he is God." And Elijah said to them, "Seize the prophets of Baal; let not one of them escape." And they seized them; and Elijah brought them down to the brook Kishon, and killed them there.

I Kings 18: 21-29, 36-40

Yahweh's prophets were more than holy men who seemed to have their God at their beck and call; they developed a vision of God as being more than a breather of fire. Genuine monotheism does not mean the belief that one god is more powerful than others. The monotheist believes that there is only one God, a universal God who rules over all lands and all peoples. The gods of other people are not just weaker, they do not even exist. Today, most people accept monotheism so readily that this conclusion seems obvious. We assume, for the most part, that the gods of other civilizations are all expressions of the same, single divine force. But in the ancient world, it was a feat of intellectual courage and spiritual insight to develop the concept of monotheism, to say that God is one.

The Hebrews did not come to this conclusion easily. David, when confronting Goliath, wanted to prove that "there is a god in Israel." He did not say that his God was everywhere. When praising Yahweh for his defeat of the Egyptians, the Hebrews said, "Who is like thee, O Lord among the gods." It would seem that their God was only stronger than Pharaoh, the god-king. Even Elijah, in his contest with Baal, asked Yahweh to "let it be known that thou are God *in Israel*" (italics not in the original). These examples show a belief in a powerful and local god, not a belief in one God.

THE DEVELOPMENT OF MONOTHEISM

Jeremiah and Amos. As time went on, the concept of monotheism emerged. The prophet Jeremiah caught a glimpse of it when he said:

> Learn not the way of the nations, nor be dismayed at the signs of the heavens because the nations are dismayed at them, for the customs of the people are false.
>
> A tree from the forest is cut down, and worked with an axe by the hands of a craftsman. Men deck it with silver and gold; they fasten it with hammer and nails so that it cannot move. Their idols are like scarecrows in a cucumber field, and they cannot speak; they have to be carried, for they cannot walk. Be not afraid of them, for they cannot do evil, neither is it in them to do good. They are both stupid and foolish; the instruction of idols is but wood. Beaten silver is brought from Tarshish, and gold from Uphaz. They are the work of the craftsman and of the hands of the goldsmith; their clothing is violet and purple; they are the work of skilled men. But the Lord is the true God; he is the living God and the everlasting King.
>
> JEREMIAH 10: 1-5, 8-10

First discovered in 1947 in caves above the Dead Sea, the "Dead Sea Scrolls" have been an invaluable archaeological find, providing additional information about the ancient Hebrew civilization.

UPI

To Jeremiah, not only was astrology ("the signs of the heavens") a false religion, but all the gods of men were unreal, capable of neither good nor evil.

The prophets did more than proclaim the fact that Yahweh was the only true God. They also turned their attention to man and his relations with his fellowmen. The prophets claimed that Yahweh was concerned about ethical and moral questions. The prophet Amos, uttering the thoughts of Yahweh, strikes this new note.

> I hate, I despise your feasts, and I take no delight in your solemn assemblies. Even though you offer me your burnt offerings and cereal offerings, I will not accept them, and the peace offering of your fatted beasts I will not look upon. Take away from me the noise of your songs; to the melody of your harps I will not listen. But let justice roll down like waters, and righteousness like an everflowing stream.
>
> Amos 5: 21-24

The Hebrews angered their God by imitating the ceremonies of other religions. Yahweh was concerned more with righteousness and justice than with sacrifices.

When Israel became a wealthy and powerful nation, its social structure lost the simplicity which it had had during the early days. Class distinctions grew up between rich and poor, and kings tended to oppress the people. This situation was not unique in the history of civilization. Social classes, inequality and injustice are common to all societies. But in the case of Israel, a striking difference can be seen. The prophets spoke out against the evils of society and the arrogance of rulers. They developed, for the first time in history, an active social conscience. They infused religion with ethics.

Samuel and Nehemiah. Even when the Hebrews first demanded a king so that they could be like other nations, the prophet Samuel had the insight to foresee the consequences of monarchy.

> These will be the ways of the king who will reign over you: he will take your sons and appoint them to his chariots and to be his horsemen, and to run before his chariots. He will take your daughters to be perfumers and cooks and bakers. He will take the best of your fields and vineyards and olive orchards and give them to his servants. He will take your menservants and maidservants, and the best of your cattle and your asses and put them to his work. He will take the tenth of your flocks, and you shall be his slaves. And in that day you will cry out because of your king, whom you have chosen for yourselves; but the Lord will not answer you in that day.
>
> I Samuel 8: 11-18

Samuel was also right about what happens when a nation becomes rich and powerful. King David had one of his soldiers killed so that he could take the man's wife. In the face of this action, the prophet Nathan exposed the wickedness of the king, and David repented. King Ahab (AY hahb) tried to take the vineyard of one of his subjects; the prophet Elijah accused him, and evil days fell upon the wicked king. The prophets portrayed a God who intervened in human affairs when social injustice was committed by one man against another. The rank of the man made little difference.

In the ancient world, it was common practice for a man to offer his land or even his children as security in order to borrow money. If the money could not be paid back, the lender could take over the property or use the children as slaves. The prophet Nehemiah (nee uh MY uh) records the situation in Israel.

> And there were those who said, "We have borrowed money for the king's tax upon our fields and our vineyards . . . we are forcing our sons and our daughters to be slaves, and some of our daughters have been enslaved; but it is not in our power to help it, for other men have our fields and vineyards."
>
> NEHEMIAH 5: 4-5

Nehemiah spoke out against this practice and envoked the power of Yahweh against this social evil.

> "Return to them this very day their fields, their vineyards, their olive orchards, and their houses, and the hundredth of money, grain, wine, and oil which you have been exacting of them!" I also shook out my lap and said, "So may God shake out every man from his house and from his labor who does not perform this promise. So may he be shaken out and emptied."
>
> NEHEMIAH 5: 11, 13

This was a revolutionary idea. In truth, ethics and morality were not invented by the Hebrews, nor was religion. However, most people in the ancient world were unable to join morality to religion successfully. Gods were concerned mainly with nature, with the changing seasons; they had little to do with the affairs of men. Of course, correct behavior was valued by all people, and in the *Negative Confession* (see pages 64-65), the Egyptians attempted to tie ethics to religion.

The Fusion of Ethics and Religion. But only among the Hebrews were ethics and religion fused, a fact which can be seen in a short Hebrew narrative appearing early in the Bible. We have already studied the Sumerian myth in which a shepherd and a farmer competed for the favor of the goddess Inanna (see page

43). The goddess chose the farmer, thereby indicating her approval of agriculture as a way of life. The following Hebrew account parallels the Sumerian myth. Both should be read and compared.

> Abel was a keeper of sheep, and Cain a tiller of the ground. In the course of time Cain brought to the Lord an offering of the fruit of the ground, and Abel brought of the firstlings of his flock and of their fat portions. And the Lord had regard for Abel and his offering, but for Cain and his offering he had no regard. So Cain was very angry, and his countenance fell. The Lord said to Cain, "Why are you angry, and why has your countenance fallen? If you do well, will you not be accepted? And if you do not do well, sin is crouching at the door; its desire is for you, but you must master it."
>
> Cain said to Abel his brother, "Let us go out into the field." And when they were in the field, Cain rose up against his brother Abel, and killed him. Then the Lord said to Cain, "Where is Abel your brother?" He said, "I do not know; am I my brother's keeper?" And the Lord said, "What have you done? The voice of your brother's blood is crying to me from the ground. And now you are cursed from the ground, which has opened its mouth to receive your brother's blood from your hand. When you till the ground, it shall no longer yield to you its strength; you shall be a fugitive and a wanderer on the earth."
>
> GENESIS 4: 2-13

The story of Cain and Abel, in the beginning, closely resembles a nature myth—a shepherd-farmer conflict—but it then goes on to probe a much deeper issue. It is an explanation of the origin of the first murder, the taking of a human life. Right in the midst of a nature story, the Hebrew writer intertwined an ethical situation. The searching question posed by Cain—"Am I my brother's keeper?"—has resounded through the ages and is still unanswered. To what extent are we responsible for others? It was the Hebrews who first posed questions such as these.

We have seen how, in the Hebrew culture, the concept of a personal single God was born—a God who transcended nature and was infused with concern for ethical behavior. There remains an important question. How did faith in Yahweh survive the destruction of the kingdom of Israel and the scattering of the Hebrew people? We will find the answer in Chapter Eleven.

Define

Yahweh
the covenant
Moses
Abraham

Review and Answer

1. What is a "transcendent god"?
2. Why is it logical that the Hebrews did not permit the practice of magic?
3. What is the connection between the separation of religion from nature and the development of true monotheism?
4. In what way was the sacrifice which Abraham was willing to make more than a personal sacrifice?
5. Illustrate the fact that the prophets used religious faith to develop a social conscience among the Hebrews.
6. According to the Hebrews, how and why did God intervene in human affairs? How do these reasons differ from those given by other peoples you have studied?

11

The Universal God of History

The decline of Israel began almost at the point of its greatest power. King Solomon, who ruled from 973 to 933 B.C., reached the pinnacle of national success by finishing the great temple in Jerusalem. But in the very building of the symbol of strength, the kingdom was weakened. Taxes had to be levied and people pressed into labor in order to build the temple of Solomon. Solomon lived a luxurious life and resistance to his rule grew, especially when he permitted the worship of many gods. During the reign of Solomon's son, rebellions broke out, and the northern tribes formed a separate state called the Kingdom of Israel. The southern tribes formed the Kingdom of Judah, retaining the city of Jerusalem as a capital. The political unity of the Hebrews was lost soon after it had been attained.

The Enslavement of Israel

Hebrew society fell prey to the social problems faced by all peoples. Political ambition and the desire for wealth caused internal friction which made the nation less able to defend itself against other nations. The two Hebrew states had to contend with the Assyrians, and in 722 B.C., the Kingdom of Israel was defeated and dismembered, with the Kingdom of Judah barely missing total destruction. Egypt roused itself to meet the Assyrian threat, and it was perhaps inevitable that the Hebrews were crushed between these two powerful states. Babylonia became powerful after the collapse of the Assyrian empire, and in 586 B.C., Judah was destroyed and the Hebrews were sent to Babylon to live in exile.

From our point of view, these events do not seem unnatural, but the prophets of Israel saw a plan at work. From their point of view, the Hebrews had indulged in unethical behavior and had worshipped gods other than Yahweh. The covenant had been broken, and therefore their God would punish them. Jeremiah described it this way.

> The sin of Judah is written with a pen of iron, with a point of diamond it is engraved on the tablet of their heart, and on the horns of their altars. Your wealth and all your treasures I will give for spoil as the price of your sin throughout all your territory. You shall loosen your hand from your heritage which I gave to you, and I will make you serve your enemies in a land which you do not know, for in my anger a fire is kindled which shall burn forever.
>
> JEREMIAH 17: 1-4

Jeremiah felt that the enslavement of Israel was not due to the fact that Assyria and Babylon were stronger but rather was caused by Yahweh, who used these nations to punish his people. If one accepts the fact of the covenant, the misfortunes of Israel can be easily explained. The Hebrews' own God planned and executed their destruction for reasons which the prophets made perfectly clear. This method of explaining events had never been used before by any ancient people. Enlil and Marduk seemed to act on their own impulses; man could not hope to explain events by looking to their gods. But by claiming that Yahweh used other nations to destroy his own people, the Hebrew prophets kept faith in him alive in the face of national disaster. In reasoning this way, the prophets were interpreting history. They believed that man could understand God through looking at the progress of human events. This was the Hebrew sense of history. It gave them an understanding of time and change which no other ancient people had.

The Hebrew Sense of History

The Egyptians had all but destroyed the concept of time and change. The unending yearly return of the Nile flood and the daily unclouded return of the sun led them to look upon the passing of events in an unhistorical way. The Babylonians also focused their attention upon the cycle of the seasons. They saw human affairs as moving in a circle, with events repeating themselves. The major religious festival for the Babylonians was the annual recitation of the creation myth; for them, Marduk created the world each year.

The Hebrews, freed from nature worship, focused their attention on historical events. They saw human affairs as moving in a straight line, from past to future. Their highest holy day was the Passover, a celebration of the deliverance from Egypt, a specific event in the past. It is also significant that their sacred book, the Bible, is not a collection of rituals but a history of their nation. This historical sense enabled the Hebrews to deal with change and to cope with events as they occurred.

Acceptance of Change. This willingness to accept and to deal with change can be seen in the following lines which describe a radical social change.

> The Lord makes poor and makes rich; he brings low, he also exalts. He raises up the poor from the dust; he lifts the needy from the ash heap, to make them sit with princes and inherit a seat of honor.
>
> I SAMUEL 2: 7-8

For other people, the structure of society had been established by the gods, never to be altered. Any kind of social or political change would confuse them. But the Hebrews could accept the fact of change, for their God not only condoned it but caused it to happen.

The prophet Isaiah's understanding of political events can be seen in the following selection in which he criticizes his rulers for attempting to seek aid from the Egyptians in order to stop the advancing Assyrians.

> Woe to those who go down to Egypt for help and rely on horses, who trust in chariots because they are many and in horsemen because they are very strong, but do not look to the Holy One of Israel or consult the Lord. And yet he is wise and brings disaster, he does not call back his words, but will arise against the house of the evil doers, and the helpers of those who work iniquity. The Egyptians are men, and not God; and their horses are flesh, and not spirit. When the Lord stretches out his hand, the helper will stumble, and he who is helped will fall, and they will all perish together.
>
> ISAIAH 31: 1-3

Both "the helper" and "he who is helped" will fall. Isaiah was able to account for and accept the tremendous changes which he foresaw, the defeat of his own land and the collapse of mighty Egypt. God was revealing himself in history through human events and no longer through nature as he had done when Elijah's sacrifice was consumed.

The Hebrews in Exile. While in exile in Babylon, some of the Hebrews believed that their God had deserted them. For others, the exile itself displayed the power of their God. Had God not used the Babylonians for his purposes? Were the Hebrews not rescued from slavery once before? The Babylonian exile proved that the religion and culture of Israel could exist outside the land of Israel, and without having a sacred temple. The exiled people found instruction in the past and hope in the future.

The prophets of the exile saw the rising power of Persia and claimed that their god was using the Persians to set them free. In reality, Cyrus of Persia did capture Babylon and did permit the Hebrews to return to Jerusalem. This is how the prophets saw these events.

> Thus says the Lord to his annointed, to Cyrus whose right hand I have grasped, to subdue nations before him and ungird the loins of kings, to open doors before him that gates may not be closed. I will go before you and level the mountains, I will break in pieces the doors of bronze and cut asunder the bars of iron . . . that you may know that it is I, the Lord, the God of Israel, who call you by your name.
>
> ISAIAH 45: 1-3

The God who was once the relatively unknown god of a small group of barbarians is now calling the Persian king by name and clearing the way for the greatest empire on earth. Here it might be well to stop calling this god Yahweh, for to the Hebrews he was not one god among many, but the only God, the Lord of all the universe.

In actual fact, Cyrus had never heard of the Hebrew God, nor did he take much notice of the Hebrews. The thoughts of the prophets were only their interpretation of events, interpretations which gave great courage to the Hebrews and strength to their religion. However, their ideas were unknown outside their own small circle. The powerful impact of Hebrew ideas came much later. This fact should give us pause. The great and controlling ideas of future centuries might well be being developed today, in a nation so small that it escapes our notice!

Hope in the Future. Even in defeat, the Hebrews looked to the future, and their prophets fashioned new ideas to meet the needs of new times. Their historical sense enabled them to generate new

Spanish Painter, Unknown, Scenes from the Creation and the Life of St. Andrew, detail: "God Creating the Animals." The Metropolitan Museum of Art, Gift of John D. Rockefeller, Jr., 1925, The Cloisters Collection.

The continuing influence of ideas which originated in the Near East is evident in the numerous paintings created centuries later. One such painting is "God Creating the Animals," a detail from a larger work by an unknown Spanish painter of the late fourteenth century.

ideas out of old ones. Their thoughts were not frozen in a timeless perfection. An image of God, often used by the prophets, was that of the potter working with the clay, which was Israel. The clay is marred, but God chooses to reform it to make a new vessel. Here is Jeremiah speaking of a *new* covenant.

> Behold, the days are coming, says the Lord, when I will make a new covenant with the house of Israel and the house of Judah, not like the covenant which I made with their fathers when I took them by the hand to bring them out of the land of Egypt, my covenant which they broke. But this is the covenant which I will make with the house of Israel after those days, says the Lord: I will put my law within them, and I will write it upon their hearts; and I will be their God, and they shall be my people. And no longer shall each man teach his neighbor and each his brother saying, "Know the Lord," for they shall all know me, from the least of them to the greatest, says the Lord; for I will forgive their iniquity, and I will remember their sin no more.
>
> JEREMIAH 31: 31-34

Jeremiah looks back to past events and forward to a new way of life involving a new concept of religion. "I will put my law within them, and I will write it upon their hearts." This idea would free religion from ritual and outward forms and make it a thing of inner conviction. Jeremiah's words imply that God wishes to continue to use his people and to forgive them in spite of their failings.

Rebirth and a New Kingdom

The kingdom of Israel was never restored for any substantial length of time; the Hebrews remained either in exile or under the rule of other people. Yet the hope of a revival of the kingdom remained. The prophet Ezekiel records a vision he had of the restoring power of God.

> The hand of the Lord was upon me, and he brought me out by the Spirit of the Lord, and set me down in the midst of the valley; it was full of bones. And he led me round among them; and behold, they were very dry. And he said to me, "Son of man, can these bones live?" And I answered, "O Lord God, thou knowest." Again he said to me, "Prophesy to these bones, hear the word of the Lord. Thus says the Lord God to these bones; Behold, I will cause breath to enter you, and you shall live. And I will lay sinews upon you, and will cause flesh to come upon you, and you shall live; and you shall know that I am the Lord."
>
> So I prophesied as I was commanded; and as I prophesied, there was a noise, and behold, a rattling, and the bones came together, bone to bone. And as I looked, there were sinews on them, and flesh had come upon them, and skin had covered them; but there was no breath in them. Then he said to me, "Prophesy to the breath, prophesy, son of man, and say to the breath, Thus says the Lord God: Come from the four winds, O breath, and breathe upon these slain, that they may live." So I prophesied as he commanded me, and the breath came into them, and they lived, and stood upon their feet, an exceedingly great host.
>
> Then he said to me, "Son of man, these bones are the whole house of Israel. Behold, they say, 'Our bones are dried up, and our hope is lost; we are clean cut off.' Therefore prophesy, and say to them, Thus says the Lord God: Behold, I will open your graves, and raise up from your graves, O my people; and I will bring you home into the land of Israel. . . ."
>
> EZEKIEL 37: 1-12

The Meaning of Rebirth. The idea of rebirth is here vividly expressed. For most of the Hebrews, this vision meant the restora-

tion of the kingdom rather than any form of personal rebirth after death. The Hebrews never developed the concept of a life after death. To them, personal salvation was found in the nation of Israel, a nation chosen by God. However, with the collapse of the kingdom and the waning of a hope of restoration, some thinkers turned to the idea of a personal rebirth. The idea of a final accounting at the end of time crept into Hebrew thinking. In the book of Daniel, one of the last books of the Bible to be written, this idea is expressed.

> And many of those who sleep in the dust of the earth shall awake, some to everlasting life, and some to shame and everlasting contempt.
>
> DANIEL 12: 2

Some Hebrews thought of rebirth as meaning not an actual geographical kingdom but a life lived under new values, under the terms of the inward covenant spoken of by Jeremiah. This would be a kind of spiritual kingdom. Gradually, the idea of a leader called a *Messiah*, who would be the ruler of the new kingdom, developed. Some saw the Messiah as a military and political leader who would establish an actual kingdom. Others saw him as a spiritual leader whose kingdom would consist of new values and a new way of life for men, a kingdom which would have no geographical bounds.

The Hebrew Influence. A much later Hebrew teacher, Jesus of Nazareth, expressed this idea when he said, "My kingdom is not of this world." A new religion, Christianity, gathered around the personality of Jesus, a Hebrew himself steeped in the ideas of the prophets. Christianity provided the religious basis of our own civilization, and so all of the ideas and concepts of ancient Israel were carried far beyond the Near East both in time and space. The prophet Isaiah looked far into the future and saw a universal role for Israel and its God. Israel would rule not through worldly power but through an empire of ideas. It would provide a God for all people and bring about the ultimate perfection of man. We shall

---

Comparing the maps on pages 21 and 164, we can see the tremendous expansion of civilization from its crude beginnings in Sumer and Egypt around 3000 B.C. A significant factor in this growth was the Phoenicians, whose trading and colonizing ventures brought civilization to barbarian peoples in Europe and northern Africa.

end this unit with Isaiah's vision of the future, a vision which contains some of our own hopes for the destiny of man.

> It shall come to pass in the latter days that the mountain of the house of the Lord shall be established as the highest of the mountains, and shall be raised above the hills; and all the nations shall flow to it, and many peoples shall come and say: "Come, let us go to the mountain of the Lord, to the house of the God of Jacob; that he may teach us his ways and that we may walk in his paths." For out of Zion shall go forth the law, and the word of the Lord from Jerusalem. He shall judge between the nations, and shall decide for many peoples; and they shall beat their swords into plowshares, and their spears into pruning hooks; nation shall not lift up sword against nation, neither shall they learn war any more.
>
> ISAIAH 2: 2-4

Define

the Passover
the Bible
Messiah

Review and Answer

1. How did the prophets keep the Hebrews true to their faith in Yahweh even in the face of national disaster?
2. How did the Hebrew concept of time and change differ from the views expressed by thinkers from other cultures?
3. What was the importance of the new covenant when God said, "I will put my law within them, and I will write it upon their hearts"?
4. In what two ways did the Hebrews interpret rebirth and the future kingdom?
5. Of all the ideas accumulated in the long history of the ancient Near East, the ideas of the Hebrews have retained their vitality and have had a powerful influence on later ages. Explain why you think this is true.

Reading V

Selections from the Old Testament

The Bible is not only our best source of information about the ancient Hebrews, but it is one of the most influential books of our civilization. Most modern ethical and moral values are drawn from the Bible, and even those people who reject formal religious beliefs must come to terms with the Bible in their rejection. So many works of art, music and literature, even down to the present, are based upon biblical ideas and events that an educated person must become familiar with portions of the Bible. Some of the stories, poetry, proverbs and moral teachings of the Old Testament are included in this selection.

Stories

Creation Stories

The Bible is the work of many authors. Even single books of the Bible represent the work of more than one writer. The fact can be seen in the two creation stories from Genesis which follow. Each of them has its own distinct style and content. It will be interesting to compare them with one another and also with the earlier Babylonian creation story (Reading IV).

GENESIS 1; 2: 1-3

In the beginning God created the heavens and the earth. The earth was without form and void, and darkness was upon the face of the deep; and the Spirit of God was moving over the face of the waters. And God said, "Let there be light"; and there was light. And God saw that the light was good; and God separated the light from the darkness. God called the light Day, and the darkness he called Night. And there was evening and there was morning one day.

And God said, "Let there be a firmament in the midst of the waters, and let it separate the waters from the waters." And God made the firmament and separated the waters which were under the firmament from the waters which were above the firmament. And it was so. And God called the firmament Heaven. And there was evening and there was morning, a second day.

And God said, "Let the waters under the heavens be gathered together in one place, and let the dry land appear." And it was so. God called the dry land Earth, and the waters that were gathered together he called Seas. And God saw that it was good. And God said, "Let the earth put forth vegetation, plants yielding seed, and fruit trees bearing fruit in which is their seed, each according to their own kinds, and trees bearing fruit in which is their seed, each according to its kind. And God saw

---

The Holy Bible, Revised Standard Version (New York: Thomas Nelson & Sons, 1953).

that it was good. And there was evening and there was morning, a third day.

And God said, "Let there be lights in the firmament of the heavens to separate the day from the night; and let them be for signs and for seasons and for days and years, and let them be lights in the firmament of the heavens to give light upon the earth." And it was so. And God made the two great lights, the greater light to rule the day, and the lesser light to rule the night; he made the stars also. And God set them in the firmament of the heavens to give light upon the earth, to rule over the day and over the night, and to separate the light from the darkness. And God saw that it was good. And there was evening and there was morning, a fourth day.

And God said, "Let the waters bring forth swarms of living creatures, and let the birds fly above the earth across the firmament of the heavens." So God created the great sea monsters and every living creature that moves, with which the waters swarm, according to their kinds, and every winged bird according to its kind. And God saw that it was good. And God blessed them, saying, "Be fruitful and multiply and fill the waters in the seas, and let birds multiply on the earth." And there was evening and there was morning, a fifth day.

And God said, "Let the earth bring forth living creatures according to their kinds: cattle and creeping things and beasts of the earth according to their kinds." And it was so. And God made the beasts of the earth according to their kinds and the cattle according to their kinds, and everything that creeps upon the ground according to its kind. And God saw that it was good.

Then God said, "Let us make man in our image, after our likeness; and let them have dominion over the fish of the sea, and over the birds of the air, and over the cattle, and over all the earth, and over every creeping thing that creeps upon the earth." So God created man in his own image, in the image of God he created him; male and female he created them. And God blessed them, and God said to them, "Be fruitful and multiply, and fill the earth and subdue it; and have dominion over the fish of the sea and over the birds of the air and over every living thing that moves upon the earth." And God said, "Behold, I have given you every plant yielding seed which is upon the face of all the earth, and every tree with seed in its fruit; you shall have them for food. And to every beast of the earth, and to every bird of the air, and to every thing that creeps on the earth, everything that has the breath of life, I have given every green plant for food." And it was so. And God saw everything that he had made, and behold, it was very good. And there was evening and there was morning, a sixth day.

Thus the heavens and the earth were finished, and all the host of them. And on the seventh day God finished his work which he had done, and he rested on the seventh day from all his work which he had done. So God blessed the seventh day and hallowed it, because on it God rested from all his work which he had done in creation.

Genesis 2: 4-24; 3

In the day that the Lord God made the earth and the heavens, when no plant of the field was yet in the earth and no herb of the field had yet sprung up—for the Lord God had not caused it to rain upon the earth, and there was no man to till the ground; but a mist went up from the earth and watered the whole face of the ground—then the Lord God formed man of dust from the ground, and breathed into his nostrils the breath of life; and man became a living being. And the Lord God planted a garden in Eden, in the east; and there he put the man whom he had formed. And out of the ground the Lord God made to grow every tree that is pleasant to the sight and good for food, the tree of life also in the midst of the garden, and the tree of the knowledge of good and evil.

The Lord God took the man and put him in the garden of Eden to till it and keep it. And the Lord God commanded the man, saying, "You may freely eat of every tree of the garden; but of the tree of the knowledge of good and evil you shall not eat, for in the day that you eat of it you shall die."

Then the Lord God said, "It is not good that the man should be alone; I will make him a helper fit for him." So out of the ground the Lord God formed every beast of the field and every bird of the air, and brought them to the man to see what he would call them; and whatever the man called every living creature, that was its name. The man gave names to all cattle, and to the birds of the air, and to every beast of the field; but for the man there was not found a helper fit for him. So the Lord God caused a deep sleep to fall upon the man, and while he slept took one of his ribs and closed up its place with flesh; and the rib which the Lord God had taken from the man he made into a woman and brought her to the man. Then the man said, "This at last is bone of my bones and flesh of my flesh; she shall be called Woman, because she was taken out of Man." Therefore a man leaves his father and his mother and cleaves to his wife, and they become one flesh. And the man and his wife were both naked, and were not ashamed.

Now the serpent was more subtle than any other wild creature that the Lord God had made. He said to the woman, "Did God say 'You shall not eat of any tree of the garden'?" And the woman said to the serpent, "We may eat of the fruit of the trees of the garden; but God said, 'You shall not eat of the fruit of the tree which is in the midst of the garden, neither shall you touch it, lest you die.'" But the serpent said to the woman, "You will not die. For God knows that when you eat of it your eyes will be opened, and you will be like God, knowing good and evil." So when the woman saw that the tree was good for food, and that it was a delight to the eyes, and that the tree was to be desired to make one wise, she took of its fruit and ate; and she also gave some to her husband, and he ate. Then the eyes of both were opened, and they knew that they were naked; and they sewed fig leaves together and made themselves aprons.

And they heard the sound of the Lord God walking in the garden in the cool of the day, and the man and his wife hid themselves from the presence of the Lord God among the trees of the garden. But the Lord God called to the man, and said to him, "Where are you?" And he said, "I heard the sound of thee in the garden, and I was afraid, because I was naked; and I hid myself." He said, "Who told you that you were naked? Have you eaten of the tree of which I commanded you not to eat?" The man said, "The woman whom thou gavest to be with me, she gave me fruit of the tree, and I ate." Then the Lord God said to the woman, "What is this that you have done?" The woman said, "The serpent beguiled me, and I ate." The Lord God said to the serpent, "Because you have done this, cursed are you above all cattle, and above all wild animals; upon your belly you shall go, and dust you shall eat all the days of your life...." To the woman he said, "I will greatly multiply your pain in childbearing; in pain you shall bring forth children, yet your desire shall be for your husband, and he shall rule over you." And to Adam he said, "Because you have listened to the voice of your wife, and have eaten of the tree of which I commanded you, 'You shall not eat of it,' cursed is the ground because of you; in toil you shall eat of it all the days of your life; thorns and thistles it shall bring forth to you; and you shall eat the plants of the field. In the sweat of your face you shall eat bread till you return to the ground, for out of it you were taken; you are dust, and to dust you shall return."

Then the Lord God said, "Behold, the man has become like one of us, knowing good and evil; and now, lest he put forth his hand and take also of the tree of life, and eat, and live for ever—therefore the Lord God sent him forth from the garden of Eden, to till the ground from which he was taken. He drove out the man; and at the east of the garden of Eden he placed the cherubim, and a flaming sword which turned every way, to guard the way to the tree of life.

The Flood Story

Even though the land of Israel was not afflicted by floods, Hebrew literature contains the story of a great flood, a story which is very much like the earlier Babylonian flood story mentioned in the text (pages 81-84). Although these two stories are similar, they contain important differences and should be compared.

GENESIS 6-8

The Lord saw that the wickedness of man was great in the earth, and that every imagination of the thoughts of his heart was only evil continually. And the Lord was sorry that he had made man on the earth, and it grieved him to his heart. So the Lord said, "I will blot out man whom I have created from the face of the ground, man and beast and creeping things and birds of the air, for I am sorry that I have made them." But Noah found favor in the eyes of the Lord.

Now the earth was corrupt in God's sight, and the earth was filled with violence. And God saw the earth, and behold, it was corrupt; for all flesh had corrupted their way upon the earth. And God said to Noah, "I have determined to make an end of all flesh; for the earth is filled with violence through them; behold, I will destroy them with the earth. Make yourself an ark of gopher wood; make rooms in the ark, and cover it inside and out with pitch. This is how you are to make it: the length of the ark three hundred cubits, its breadth fifty cubits, and its height thirty cubits. Make a roof for the ark and finish it to a cubit above; and set the door of the ark in its side; make it with lower, second, and third decks. For behold, I will bring a flood of waters upon the earth, to destroy all flesh in which is the breath of life from under heaven; everything that is on the earth shall die. But I will establish my covenant with you; and you shall come into the ark, you, your sons, your wife and your sons' wives with you. And of every living thing of all flesh, you shall bring two of every sort into the ark, to keep them alive with you; they shall be male and female. Of the birds according to their kinds, of every creeping thing of the ground according to its kind, two of every sort shall come in to you, to keep them alive. Also take with you every sort of food that is eaten, and store it up; and it shall serve as food for you and for them." Noah did this; he did all that God commanded him.

In the six hundredth year of Noah's life, in the second month, on the seventeenth day of the month, on that day all the fountains of the great deep burst forth, and the windows of the heavens were opened. And rain fell upon the earth forty days and forty nights. The waters prevailed and increased greatly upon the earth; and the ark floated on the face of the waters. And the waters prevailed so mightily upon the earth that all the high mountains under the whole heaven were covered; the waters prevailed above the mountains, covering them fifteen cubits deep. And all flesh died that moved upon the earth, birds, cattle, beasts, all swarming creatures that swarm upon the earth, and every man; everything on the dry land in whose nostrils was the breath of life died. He blotted out every living thing that was upon the face of the ground, man and animals and creeping things and birds of the air; they were blotted out from the earth. Only Noah was left, and those that were with him in the ark. And the waters prevailed upon the earth a hundred and fifty days.

But God remembered Noah and all the beasts and all the cattle that were with him in the ark. And God made a wind blow over the earth, and the waters subsided; the fountains of the deep and the windows of the heavens were closed, the rain from the heavens was restrained, and the waters receded from the earth continually. At the end of a hundred and fifty days the waters had abated; and in the seventh month, on the seventeenth day of the month, the ark came to rest upon the mountains of Ararat.

At the end of forty days Noah opened the window of the ark which he had made, and sent forth a raven; and it went to and fro until the waters were dried up from the earth. Then he sent forth a dove from him, to see if the waters had subsided from the face of the ground; but the dove found no place to set her foot, and she returned to him to the ark, for the waters were still on the face of the whole earth. So he put forth his hand and took her and brought her into the ark with him. He waited another seven days, and again sent forth the dove out of the ark; and the dove came back to him in the evening, and lo, in her mouth a freshly plucked olive leaf; so Noah knew that the waters had subsided from the earth. Then he waited another seven days, and sent forth the dove; and she did not return to him any more.

Then God said to Noah, "Go forth from the ark, you and your wife, and your sons and your sons' wives with you. Bring forth with you every living thing that is with you of all flesh . . . that they may breed abundantly on the earth, and be fruitful and multiply upon the earth." Then Noah built an altar to the Lord, and took of every clean animal and of every clean bird, and offered burnt offerings on the altar. And when the Lord smelled the pleasing odor, the Lord said in his heart, "I will never again curse the ground because of man, for the imagination of man's heart is evil from his youth; neither will I ever again destroy every living creature as I have done. While the earth remains, seedtime and harvest, cold and heat, summer and winter, day and night, shall not cease."

The Division of Mankind

GENESIS 11:1-9

Now the whole earth had one language and few words. And as men migrated in the east, they found a plain in the land of Shinar and settled there. And they said to one another, "Come, let us make bricks, and burn them thoroughly." And they had brick for stone, and bitumen for mortar. Then they said, "Come, let us build ourselves a city, and a tower with its top in the heavens, and let us make a name for ourselves, lest we be scattered abroad upon the face of the whole earth." And the Lord came down to see the city and the tower, which the sons of men had built. And the Lord said, "Behold, they are one people, and they have all one language; and this is only the beginning of what they will do; and nothing that they propose to do will now be impossible for them. Come, let us go down, and there confuse their language, that they may not understand one another's speech." So the Lord scattered them abroad from there over the face of all the earth, and they left off building the city. Therefore its name was called Babel, because there the Lord scattered them abroad over the face of all the earth.

Poetry

A poetic impulse runs through the Bible, and many examples of poetry can be taken from it. What follows here is a selection of six poems, called Psalms, which display some of the values held by the Hebrews. Psalm 1 points out the way of the good man. Psalms 19 and 139 proclaim the power and transcendence of God, yet at the same time show the closeness of God to man. Psalm 104 is a nature poem showing God as the lord of physical creation, whereas Psalm 137 is a historical poem dealing with a specific event, the enslavement of the Hebrews by

SELECTIONS FROM THE OLD TESTAMENT 173

the Babylonians. Psalm 98 shows the full scope of the Hebrew concept of God in which both human events and the forces of nature respond to the divine power.

Psalm 1

> Blessed is the man who walks not in the counsel of the wicked,
> nor stands in the way of sinners, nor sits in the seat of the scoffers;
> But his delight is in the law of the Lord,
> and on his law he meditates day and night.
> He is like a tree planted by streams of water, that yields its
> fruit in its season, and its leaf does not wither.
> In all that he does, he prospers.
> The wicked are not so, but are like chaff which the wind drives away.
> Therefore the wicked will not stand in the judgement,
> nor sinners in the congregation of the righteous; for
> the Lord knows the way of the righteous, but the way of
> the wicked will perish.

Psalm 19

> The heavens are telling the glory of God; and the firmament
> proclaims his handiwork.
> Day to day pours forth speech, and night to night declares knowledge.
> There is no speech, nor are there words; their voice is not heard;
> yet their voice goes out through all the earth, and their
> words to the end of the world.
> In them he has set a tent for the sun, which comes forth like a
> bridegroom leaving his chamber, and like a strong man runs
> its course with joy.
> Its rising is from the end of the heavens, and its circuit to the
> end of them; and there is nothing hid from its heat.
> The law of the Lord is perfect, reviving the soul; the testimony
> of the Lord is sure, making wise the simple; the precepts of
> the Lord are right, rejoicing the heart; the commandment of the
> Lord is pure, enlightening the eyes; the fear of the Lord is clean,
> enduring for ever; the ordinances of the Lord are true, and
> righteous altogether.
> More to be desired are they than gold, even much fine gold;
> sweeter also than honey and drippings of the honeycomb.
> Moreover by them is thy servant warned; in keeping them there
> is great reward.
> But who can discern his errors? Clear thou me from hidden faults.
> Keep back thy servant also from presumptuous sins; let them
> not have dominion over me!
> Then I shall be blameless, and innocent of great transgression.
> Let the words of my mouth and the meditation of my heart be
> acceptable in thy sight, O Lord, my rock and my redeemer.

Psalm 139

O Lord, thou hast searched me and known me!

Thou knowest when I sit down and when I rise up; thou discernest my thoughts from afar.

Thou searchest out my path and my lying down, and are acquainted with all my ways.

Even before a word is on my tongue, lo, O Lord, thou knowest it altogether.

Thou dost beset me behind and before, and layest thy hand upon me.

Such knowledge is too wonderful for me; it is high, I cannot attain it.

Wither shall I go from thy Spirit? Or wither shall I flee from thy presence?

If I ascend to heaven, thou art there! If I make my bed in Sheol,* thou art there!

If I take the wings of the morning and dwell in the uttermost parts of the sea, even there thy hand shall lead me, and thy right hand shall hold me.

If I say, "Let only darkness cover me, and the light about me be night," even the darkness is not dark to thee, the night is bright as the day; for darkness is as light with thee.

For thou didst form my inward parts, thou didst knit me together in my mother's womb.

I praise thee, for thou art fearful and wonderful.

Psalm 104

Bless the Lord, O my soul! O Lord my God, thou art very great!

Thou art clothed with honor and majesty,
> who coverest thyself with light as with a garment,
> who hast stretched out the heavens like a tent,
> who hast laid the beams of thy chambers on the waters,
> who makes the clouds thy chariot, who fliest on the wings of the wind,
> who makes the winds thy messengers, fire and flame thy ministers.

Thou didst set the earth on its foundations, so that it should never be shaken.

Thou didst cover it with the deep as with a garment; the waters stood above the mountains.

At thy rebuke they fled; at the sound of thy thunder they took to flight.

The mountains rose, the valleys sank down to the place which thou didst appoint for them.

Thou didst set a bound which they should not pass, so that they might not again cover the earth.

Thou makes springs gush forth in the valleys; they grow between the hills, they give drink to every beast of the field; the wild asses quench their thirst.

---

* The land of the dead.

By them the birds of the air have their habitation; they sing
   among the branches.
From thy lofty abode thou waterest the mountains; the earth is
   satisfied with the fruit of thy work.
Thou dost cause the grass to grow for the cattle, and plants for
   man to cultivate, that he may bring forth food from the earth,
   and wine to gladden the heart of man, oil to make his face
   shine, and bread to strengthen man's heart.
The trees of the Lord are watered abundantly, the cedars of
   Lebanon which he planted.
In them the birds build their nests; the stork has her home in
   the fir trees.
The high mountains are for the wild goats; the rocks are a refuge
   for the badgers.
Thou has made the moon to mark the seasons; the sun knows its time
   for setting.
Thou makest darkness, and it is night when all the beasts of the
   forest creep forth.
The young lions roar for their prey, seeking their food from God.
When the sun rises, they get them away and lie down in their dens.
Man goes forth to his work and to his labor until the evening.
O Lord, how manifold are thy works! In wisdom hast thou
   made them all; the earth is full of thy creatures.
Yonder is the sea, great and wide, which teems with things
   innumerable, living things both small and great.
There go the ships, and Leviathan which thou didst form to sport in it.
These all look to thee, to give them their food in due season.
When thou givest to them, they gather it up; when thou openest
   thy hand, they are filled with good things.
When thou hidest thy face, they are dismayed; when thou takest
   away their breath, they die and return to their dust.
When thou sendest forth thy Spirit, they are created; and thou
   renewest the face of the ground.
May the glory of the Lord endure for ever, may the Lord rejoice
   in his works, who looks on the earth and it trembles, who
   touches the mountains and they smoke!
I will sing to the Lord as long as I live; I will sing praise
   to my God while I have being.
May my meditation be pleasing to him, for I rejoice in the Lord.
Let sinners be consumed from the earth, and let the wicked be no
   more!
Bless the Lord, O my soul!
Praise the Lord.

Psalm 137

By the waters of Babylon, there we sat down and wept, when we
   remembered Zion.
On the willows there we hung up our lyres.

For there our captors required of us songs, and our tormentors, mirth,
    saying, "Sing us one of the songs of Zion!"
How shall we sing the Lord's song in a foreign land?
If I forget you, O Jerusalem, let my right hand wither!
Let my tongue cleave to the roof of my mouth, if I do not remember
    you, if I do not set Jerusalem above my highest joy!
Remember, O Lord, against the Edomites the day of Jerusalem, how
    they said, "Rase it, rase it! Down to its foundations!"
O daughter of Babylon, you devastator! Happy shall he be who
    requites you with what you have done to us!
Happy shall he be who takes your little ones and dashes them against
    the rock!

Psalm 98

O sing to the Lord a new song, for he has done marvelous things!
His right hand and his holy arm have gotten him victory.
The Lord has made known his victory, he has revealed his
    vindication in the sight of the nations.
He has remembered his steadfast love and faithfulness to the
    house of Israel.
All the ends of the earth have seen the victory of our God.
Make a joyful noise to the Lord all the earth; break forth into
    joyous song and sing praises!
Sing praises to the Lord with the lyre, with the lyre and the sound
    of melody!
With trumpets and the sound of the horn make a joyful noise before
    the King, the Lord!
Let the sea roar, and all that fills it; the world and those who
    dwell in it!
Let the floods clap their hands; let the hills sing for joy together
    before the Lord, for he comes to rule the earth.
He will judge the world with righteousness, and the peoples
    with equity.

Proverbs

Almost every civilization has developed the literary form of the proverb, a short piece of instruction containing everything from moral teaching to practical advice. We have already seen some of the Sumerian proverbs (pages 48-49). The following Hebrew proverbs not only tell us about the values held by the ancient Hebrews, but speak to human situations for all times.

Happy is the man who finds wisdom, and the man who gets understanding, for the gain from it is better than gain from silver and its profit better than gold.
A prudent man conceals his knowledge, but fools proclaim their folly.
He who troubles his household will inherit wind.
A soft answer turns away wrath, but a harsh word stirs up anger.

He who mocks the poors insults his Maker; he who is glad at calamity will not go unpunished.

He who walks with wise men becomes wise, but the companion of fools will suffer harm.

A good name is to be chosen rather than great riches, and favor is better than silver or gold.

A cheerful heart is a good medicine, but a downcast spirit dries up the bones.

A man's spirit will endure sickness; but a broken spirit who can bear?

A rebuke goes deeper into a man of understanding than a hundred blows into a fool.

He who is slow to anger is better than the mighty, and he who rules his spirit than he who takes a city.

He who is kind to the poor lends to the Lord, and he will repay him for his deed.

He who belittles his neighbor lacks sense, but a man of understanding remains silent.

The rich and poor meet together, the Lord is the maker of them all.

Do not boast about tomorrow, for you do not know what a day may bring forth. Let another praise you, and not your own mouth; a stranger and not your own lips.

Better is open rebuke than hidden love. Faithful are the wounds of a friend; profuse are the kisses of an enemy.

Like a lame man's legs, which hang useless, is a proverb in the mouth of fools.

Sentiment

The two final selections illustrate the variety of sentiment contained in the Old Testament. The first, from the Book of Isaiah, sings of the transcendent power of God and of the strength he imparts to man. The second, from the Book of Ecclesiastes, is deeply pessimistic in tone and speaks of the lack of purpose in the world. Both can be seen as a mirror of the human soul, recording both the heights and depths of human experience.

Isaiah 40: 6-8, 28-31.

All flesh is grass, and all its beauty is like the flower of the field.

The grass withers, the flower fades, when the breath of the Lord blows upon it; surely the people is grass.

The grass withers, the flower fades; but the word of our God will stand for ever.

The Lord is the everlasting God, the Creator of the ends of the earth.

He does not faint or grow weary, his understanding is unsearchable.

He gives power to the faint, and to him who has no might he increases strength.

Even youths shall faint and be weary, and young men shall fall
  exhausted; but they who wait for the Lord shall renew their
  strength, they shall mount up with wings like eagles, they shall run
  and not be weary, they shall walk and not faint.

ECCLESIASTES 1: 3-11, 16-18.

What does man gain by all the toil at which he toils under the sun?

A generation goes, and a generation comes, but the earth remains
  for ever.

The sun rises and the sun goes down, and hastens to the place where
  it rises.

The wind blows to the south, and goes round to the north;
  round and round goes the wind, and on its circuits the wind returns.

All streams run to the sea, but the sea is not full; to the
  place where streams flow, there they flow again.

All things are full of weariness; a man cannot utter it;
  the eye is not satisfied with seeing, nor the ear filled with hearing.

What has been is what will be, and what has been done is what
  will be done; and there is nothing new under the sun.

Is there a thing of which it is said, "See, this is new?"

It has been already, in the ages before us.

There is no remembrance of former things, nor will there be any
  remembrance of later things yet to happen among those who come
  after.

I said to myself, "I have acquired great wisdom, surpassing all who
  were over Jerusalem before me; and my mind has had great experience of wisdom and knowledge." And I applied my mind to know
  wisdom and to know madness and folly. I perceived that this also is
  but a striving after wind. For in much wisdom is much vexation,
  and he who increases knowledge increases sorrow.

Shown here is a close-up of the ancient Hebrew language from which the Old Testament was translated. This was one of the earliest languages to use an alphabet.

Wide World Photos

Epilogue: The Legacy of the Near East

Many thousands of years have been covered in these five units. We have traced the development of civilization through one half of its existence so far on earth. The focus of this book has been upon one period of time and on one area of the earth. We must remember that it was not only in the Near East that civilization was created. Archaeological evidence shows that the *earliest* civilization was in Mesopotamia, but men in other parts of the world also attained this level of development. The Indus River valley in western India provided the environment for another civilization which served as the basis of later developments in India and Southeast Asia. In the valley of the Yellow River in China, another civilization grew up which is equally important for the history of East Asia. Civilization was also created in South and Central America, although this early civilization was almost totally destroyed by European settlers.

The histories of different civilizations roughly parallel each other. About the time that the prophets of Israel were shaping the religious ideas of the Hebrews, in India a religious thinker by the name of Buddha was developing ideas which have had a great influence upon the culture of the East. Buddhism is a major world religion today. In China, during the fifth century B.C., a thinker named Confucius was developing a new view of life which has shaped much of the thought of the East. Even the extinct civilization of early America has left its influences upon modern Latin America.

For a long time, distance separated these distinct civilizations from each other, but during our own age, we are witnessing an encounter of civilizations. People with widely different values and habits are coming into contact with each other. The encounter is often violent, and it is always fraught with misunderstandings. We should realize that people are the way they are because of inherited patterns of behavior and thinking, patterns which have been developed over the centuries. For this reason, it is essential that the educated person of the twentieth century be aware of the history and structure of his own and of other civilizations.

For us in the Western world, the ideas generated in the ancient Near East are important. The basic tools of living were developed there—not just physical tools such as axes, levers, metallurgy and architecture, but social tools such as languages, laws and religious beliefs. Our study of the Near East has ended at about 500 B.C. This date has been chosen not because the creativity of this period stopped at that time, but because around the fourth century B.C., other people took the initiative and seemed to overshadow the Near East. These people were the Greeks and Romans, subjects of another book. However, the creativity of the Near East remained. Out of the ideas created there, especially those of the Hebrews, several world religions grew and spread around the globe. No less than three higher religions have sprung from the Near East—Judaism, Christianity and Islam.

How should we assess this long period of human history? Having studied this period, what can we say about the construction of human civilization? In Chapter One, we divided the culture of man into four elements. It might be wise, in conclusion, to look briefly at these four elements once again.

Achievements in Controlling Nature

In studying man's *control of his environment,* we have seen how, for almost all of his history, man lived as a hunter, snatching what he could from nature in order to fulfill his basic needs. One of the most important of these thefts was fire, a source of energy which has given man almost limitless power. But the discovery of farming the soil and domesticating animals—what we have called the *Neolithic Revolution*—was perhaps the most significant step which man has taken throughout his entire life on earth. This discovery gave him the possibility of surplus food and of leisure time with which to devote his energies to new pursuits. The result was a long succession of inventions.

Yet, the discovery of agriculture has a deeper significance. It gave to man a new way of viewing his environment. With it, he was able to exploit nature in a systematic manner rather than to loot it when he needed something. This new perspective has been, and remains, the basis of man's power over his environment. At first, the earth yielded only food, but continued probing on the part of man produced much more. Iron, coal and petroleum still form the basis of our modern industrial society. Even electric and atomic energy are the result of using nature in a way developed by farmers some ten thousand years ago in the Near East. The energy of fire, when applied to the resources of the earth, is at the root of modern man's control of his environment.

The physical power of twentieth century man is far greater than that of the ancient Egyptian, but the basic sources of that power, and the fundamental method of obtaining it, were present on the banks of the Nile. When we think of the massive pyramids of Egypt, the siege towers of the Assyrians and the Persian King's Highway, we must remember that these things were all constructed without the aid of steam or electrical power. The technological accomplishment of the peoples of the Near East was no less than is ours today.

Achievements in Communication

In the area of *communication*, it is thought that man began as a grunting animal. During the period we have studied, he developed not only an elaborate written language of shapes and pictures, but he also created the concept of an alphabet, which provided a flexible and efficient instrument of communication. Most of what we learn today comes through the medium of the written word, and the very alphabet we use in the construction of our language can be traced back to ancient Phoenicia. Today we can communicate more thoughts more rapidly than did ancient men, but it is questionable whether or not the quality of our communication is better than theirs.

With the continued use of films and television, some people think that visual communication will displace the written word. Since man can continually change his cultural tools, it could be possible that alphabetic writing is only one phase in man's continuing development. In the distant future, forms, symbols and electrical impulses might well take the place of our written word.

Achievements in Cooperation

In the area of *cooperation*, the accomplishment of man in the Near East was extensive. Man moved from living in small tribes to living in large empires. Here it might be valuable to sketch out the evolution of man's political creativity.

A *tribe* is a mobile organization of people usually consisting of a group of loosely joined families. It is a flexible form of government, one which seems designed for people on the move. Paleolithic man lived in tribes, and pastoral people such as the Hebrews usually had a tribal organization. It is an adequate form of government for certain conditions but one which lacks stability; it can be easily broken up.

A *village* is a small community usually resting on an economic basis of fishing or farming. It represents a fairly stable form of government based on a way of life requiring a settled existence. Members of a village are usually engaged in the same or similar kinds of work. In a farming village, most men would be either farmers or makers of agricultural tools. This form of organization exists today in rural areas, and it was the prevailing political unit in the ancient world.

The *city-state*, created by the Sumerians in Mesopotamia, is a larger unit than the village and was made possible by rapid economic growth. In Mesopotamia, a surplus supply of food enabled a number of people to specialize in many different occupations. In a city, there could be scholars, merchants, craftsmen, priests and soldiers. A city-state is a small but powerful political unit encompassing a wide variety of people living in close proximity. It provides a creative atmosphere, and it was in the early cities that civilization was created.

A *nation* is much larger than a city and sometimes consists of several cities including the land between them. The development of national government permitted man to control and concentrate power. The Egyptians used this kind of government and also developed the concept of a bureaucracy. As we have seen, a bureaucracy is an organization of men that provides law and order over an area which no single ruler could control. The pyramids are the best evidence of the effectiveness of Egyptian social and political organization.

An *empire*, a collection of nations, is the largest form of government yet devised. In the ancient world, the Persians perfected this form of government. It was a political organization capable of providing unity, stability and easy communication throughout a very large area. All empires are built by force, but some have permitted a good deal of freedom for the subject peoples. Others have attempted to suppress all freedom and diversity within them. Imperial rule, if exercised wisely, can provide law, order and peace.

The progress of ancient man in the area of cooperation might be seen if we were to compare the roles of a Paleolithic chieftain with that of a Persian satrap. The chieftain would lead his people on the hunt, shouting directions to them, pointing them toward the kill, toward the source of their livelihood. The satrap would oversee a large province, collect taxes, appoint assistants and write dispatches. In fact, the Persian official would do just about everything that a modern official would. This fact raises a question. Have we improved upon the political creations of the ancients? Governments may have more to do today, but few states are as large as was the Persian empire. Problems of maintaining order and making war were faced by the ancients, but today's world is still a collection of separate nations which still make war on each other.

There is one element of human cooperation which was unknown to ancient man. Society in the Near East made no provision for individual involvement in the process of government. The concepts of democracy and of individual freedom were not grasped in the ancient Near East. The prevailing form of government was absolute monarchy, and the structure of society was unchangeable. Only in Israel do we find a different notion, for there the prophets openly urged social change, and even a shepherd boy could become a king. For the most part, however, the idea of an open society and individual freedom was unimaginable in the Near East.

Achievements in the World of Ideas

It is through *the use of his mind and spirit* that man's cultural achievement can be best displayed. The basic source of man's distinction is his ability to conceptualize. Only man, among the animals, is able to abstract the principles of things and apply them as he sees fit. In Chapter One, we saw how a human being could grasp the principle of leverage and use this concept to build a machine. This ability freed him from a process of trial and error and taught him to use his mind rather than his instinct. This conceptualizing ability enabled man to have a world of ideas, to move in a plane of reality which was not physical. Often these ideas were used in the physical world, such as the concept of leverage which built the pyramids. Electricity and atomic energy were first conceived in the minds of individual thinkers. All of man's inventions have stemmed from his ability to think about and conceive things which he cannot see immediately before him.

Not all of man's ideas were used to create machines, and not all of his concepts were technological ones. Purely spiritual and moral ideas were also born in his mind. It is in this particular area of culture that the ancient Near East was so very creative. The technology of ancient society is primitive when compared to that of a modern factory, but the religious, ethical and moral insights of the ancients are equal, if not superior, to ours. In many cases, they are the same. Man's ability to learn about himself by looking at his past actions is an important source of knowledge. The concept of time and change—the idea of history—was born in the ancient Near East. Without it, a person would be unable to understand this book; in fact, it could never have been written.

From the time that man became conscious of his own identity and of his distinctness from the rest of nature, he became aware of the need for a spiritual framework in which to live. Early man used religion to control and to gain unity with the powerful forces of nature surrounding him. Religion is designed to give man a place and purpose in the universe and to provide him with the spiritual strength to overcome his human weaknesses. Modern civilization is not permeated with religion as was the culture of the ancient Near East. Not all people today pose problems in religious terms, but the problems remain, and for many individuals, psychoanalysis performs the role which religion did in earlier times.

Early religion centered around the basic facts of human existence, such as birth, growth, sustenance, and death. Early man's responses to these circumstances may appear somewhat simple-minded to us, but these events are still powerful forces in human society. The problems and pressures surrounding teenagers show that "coming of age" is still a significant problem in human life. With the creation of civilization, man produced a complex society and separated himself even further from nature. The more he learned and the more power he gained, the more questions and problems there were. The myths of Near Eastern civilizations were elaborate, sophisticated devices for explaining the universe and expressing man's hopes and fears. The annual reciting of the creation myth in Babylonia confirmed the people's faith, not only in Marduk, but in the everlasting order of the universe. Belief in nature gods and the construction of mythical tales infused the universe with a personality, made it human and so brought it within the understanding of man.

Civilization also brought about rapid change. The "sense of the group" which had existed in earlier times weakened, and men had to develop new rules for living together as individuals. Hammurabi's Code is one such example, but this is a set of rather mechanical rules to govern specific conditions. Man needed more general rules and values, principles of behavior which apply to all kinds of situations. He faced problems of ethics and morality. He had to cope with the passions and prejudices of his own human personality; as human freedom expands, the pressures become stronger.

In order to deal with ethical and moral questions, man had to gain an insight into the sources of human conduct. Glimmers of this insight can be seen in some of the Egyptian and Hebrew proverbs. The *Negative Confession* shows that men were concerned about questions of behavior. Even the rather happy "Story of Sinuhe" displays some of the hopes and fears of an individual man. The "Righteous Sufferer" is an example of a man who is dissatisfied with the accepted pattern of life and who attempts to find a new basis for human conduct. The epic figure of Gilgamesh represents man's attempt to gain knowledge of himself and of the purpose of life. In a sense, we can view the entire Hebrew Bible as an attempt to understand the nature of man. In the words of the prophet Jeremiah, "The heart is deceitful above all things, and desperately corrupt; who can understand it?"

The Price of Progress

Looking at man in the ancient Near East and comparing him with modern man, can we say that the history of man shows any progress? Although we continually see vast technological improvements all around us, is the heart of modern man less "deceitful" or less "desperately corrupt" than that of ancient man? Can we understand "the heart" with its ethical and moral problems any better than did the people we have been studying? Do improvements really serve to improve the total condition of man, or do they merely bring new problems with them?

The discovery of agriculture was a great step forward, but at the same time, this very discovery took away from man some of the strength, vigor and mobility which he had had when he was a hunter. The attaining of a surplus supply of food gave man power and freedom, but it also made professional armies and organized warfare possible. The invention of written language seems to have been a great mark of progress, but it brought about a division within human society; those who could read were separated from those who could not. Even the invention of coinage made it easier for some men to hoard wealth and to dominate those who had no money.

The concept of monotheism brought about a new problem. The belief in one true God produced a desire to convert all people to his worship. In such a way, the religious war was born, a kind of conflict which is unknown among polytheistic people. In our own time, the invention of labor-saving machines has produced unemployment, one of the great sources of social discontent. Even the discovery of wonder drugs, which enable people to escape fatal diseases, has led to population pressure and the need to provide a useful function for older people.

Ancient man saw clearly the price which was always paid for progress. In the epic of Gilgamesh, when Enkidu learned the arts of civilization, he lost the harmony he had had with nature, and he became weak. When Adam and Eve gained knowledge of good and evil through eating the forbidden fruit, they lost their innocence and had to face a multitude of problems. In the words of the Bible, "In much wisdom is much vexation, and he who increases knowledge increases sorrow."

Yet to most of us, progress seems worth the price, and we tend to feel that our way of life is better than that lived by men in ancient times. We feel this way when we contemplate an Egyptian exhausting his energies to help build a pyramid, a Babylonian priest trying to predict the future by looking in the liver of an animal, a Persian subject paying a tax he had not voted for, or a Canaanite farmer prostrating himself before an altar of Baal in order to insure the growth of his crops. To us, such activities appear silly and perhaps brutal, but ancient man understood his universe. He talked to the stars and rested secure in the constant rhythm of nature. The sense of past and future, the notion of change, seems to make us superior to the ancient man trapped in the cycle of the seasons. But, we are very much aware of ghastly mistakes which have been made in the past, and we are often anxious about the future. Before there was any concept of time and change, there was no anxiety of this sort.

We generally have an excellent control over our environment. No priestly caste tells us how to please the gods of sky and soil, no ruler insists that the security of our nation depends upon the building of his tomb. We are quite free from many of the restraints placed upon ancient man, but this very freedom has created new problems which press upon us with far greater force than they did upon the ancients. For example, each of us must select one college or career out of many. We must, in a democracy, have an informed opinion on political, economic and social issues. Also, in many situations, we must make personal moral decisions without the aid of clear-cut rules. The price of freedom is high.

Is there such a thing as progress? The art of the ancient Egyptians or even of Paleolithic hunters is not inferior to ours. Perhaps it is through art that we can see the equality of all men regardless of where or when they lived. Man remains the same; his cultural forms change. His problems are sometimes different, but no civilization has more or less of them. If we could stand in the future and look at our own times the way we have been looking at the ancient Near East, we might learn a great deal about ourselves. As this is impossible, we should look at ourselves in the same way that we have looked at the peoples described in this book. The study of history enables us to see man from many points of view. In looking at man in any point of time, we are looking at ourselves.

INDEX

INDEX

Abel, 156
Abraham, 122, 149-50
Achaemenid dynasty, 132
Aegean Sea, 89
Agriculture, 21, 43, 49. *See also* Farming
Ahab, King, 155
Ahura Mazda, 137, 138
Akhnaton, and Aton, 144; attempt at monotheism, 146; deeds of, 98-99; god of, 147; and Hebrews, 101-102. *See also* Amenhotep
Alphabet, and civilization, 131; importance of, 115-19, 124; social effects of, 117, 118
Amenhotep, 97-98. *See also* Akhnaton
Amon, 96
Amon-Re, 96, 97
Amos, 145, 153-54
Anat, 119-20
Anthropologist, cultural, 6; definition, 2; goals of, 11; physical, 5
Anthropology, 2
Anu, 43, 78
Archaeologist, 17, 87, 144
Archaeology, 17, 57, 88-89
Architecture, 22, 126, 127
Art, Assyrian, 127-28; Cretan, 89-90; Egyptian, 92, 98; as element of culture, 11; paleolithic, 17; under Semites, 76
Assyria, 126-29, 158, 160
Astrology, 84-86, 154
Aton, 98, 99-101, 144
Atonist movement, 97-99, 102
Atum, 61
Avesta, 138

Baal, 119-20, 151
Babylon, conquest by Cyrus, 134; development of, 76-77; and Egypt, 96; Hebrews in, 161; and importance of Marduk, 79; and Persian success, 135
Babylonia, and afterlife, 84; astrology in, 84-86; civilization, 85; creation story, 79, 107-11; culture, 86; and divination, 85; effect on Assyria, 126; empire of, 76-86; evening hymn, 85; fall of, 85; gods, 146; government, 76-77; and Hebrews, 158; Hittite invasion of, 86; laws, 77-79; literature, 79; mythology, 79, 86; sense of time, 159; society, 76, 78
Barter, 130
Bible, and Egyptian proverbs, 94; God in, 145; as Hebrew history, 122, 160; reliability, 144. *See also* individual books

Britain, 116
Britons, 87
Bronze, 22, 115
Bryan, William Jennings, 23
Bureaucracy, 55-56, 59
Byblos, 96, 116

Cadiz, 116
Cain, 156
Cambyses, 139
Canaan, conquest of, 150; gods, 151; Hebrews in, 121-22, 144, 147; myths, 119-21; nature of civilization, 119-20; religion, 119
Carthage, 116
Cheops, 57
Christianity, 165
City-state, 37
Civilization, Babylonian, 85; and coinage, 131; contributions of Phoenicians, 119; definition, 26; effect of alphabet on, 117-18; Egyptian, 91, 102; elements of, 26-28; first, 26; and formation of classes, 40; impact of, 28-31; impact of Hebrews on, 123, 144; impact of iron on, 115; and laws, 78; and leisure time, 47; *map*, 20, 164; Mesopotamian, 36, 85, 102; and polytheism, 146; spread of, 76, 131; Sumerian, 36; transmission by Crete, 90; and war, 77, 128; Western, 26
Codification, 78
Coinage, 129-31
Colonies, 116
Communication, 9-10, 27
Cooperation, 10, 23, 27
Copper, 22
Cosmogony, 79
Cosmology, 42-44
Covenant, breaking of, 151, 159; definition, 147; and faith, 149; and monotheism, 146-51; new, 162, 165
Crete, 88-90
Croesus, 131, 134
Cro-Magnon man, 3
Culture, agrarian, 21; and assimilation, 87-88; Babylonian, 86; definition, 6, 7-8; development of, 5-8; elements of, 8-13; evolution of, 90; Hittite, 86; Israel's, 161; Neolithic, 19-26; Paleolithic, 13-18; Sumerian, 38-42
Cuneiform, 39, 126
Cyrus, advice from Croesus, 134; feats of, 132-34; and gods, 146; and Hebrews, 161; importance of, 137

190

Daedalus, 89
Daniel, 165
Darius, 139-40
David, attitude toward God, 152; and conquest of Canaan, 122; and Goliath, 148; as king, 155
Death, and Egyptian beliefs, 59, 63-67, 93; and Hebrews, 165; in nature religions, 23; and primitive religion, 16; in religion, 63
Divination, 85
Domestication, 21
Dynasty, 54

Earth, 2
Earth mother, 23
Ecclesiastes, 178
Economics, 11
Economy, 8
Education, 39
Egypt, and aid for Israel, 160; art, 92; art and Atonist movement, 98; Assyrian invasion of, 127; and Assyrians, 158; basis for wealth, 97; and Canaan, 119; civilization in, 67, 90, 102; concept of death, 93; concept of life, 93-95; concept of time, 159; and Cretan civilization, 88; and cultural exchange, 97; Eighteenth Dynasty, 96; in first millennium B.C., 126; geography, 52-54; gods, 96, 146; government, 54-57, 91; Hebrews in, 122, 150, 160; and Hebrew strength, 123; and Hittites, 98, 101; and Hyksos invasion, 95-96; ideals, 94; Imperial Period, 95; invasion by nomads, 91; isolation of, 53-54, 60; literature, 67; Middle Kingdom, 91; and morality and ethics, 65; multiplicity of thought, 91-95; Old Kingdom, 56, 91; Persian conquest, 134, 139; and Persian success, 135-37; political system, 53; proverbs, 67, 93-94; religion, 61-67, 91-92, 97-102, 137, 146; religion and reform, 97-99; and sense of history, 93; social system, 53, 55, 56, 57, 77; and Syrian cities, 116; trade, 130; values, 93; view of universe, 92-93; and war, 128; writing, 56-57, 117
Elijah, and Ahab, 155; and monotheism, 152; as prophet, 151-52; Yahweh's appearance to, 145, 146
Enki, 43, 44
Enkidu, 79, 80, 81, 84
Enlil, actions of, 159; compared with Aton, 98; in Hammurabi's Code, 78; in myth, 43-44; nature of, 144; as Sumerian god, 43; in Sumerian lament, 41
Environment, 8-9
Eolith, 13

Epic, 79
Ethics, definition, 11; Egyptian, 65; fusion with religion, 155-56; Hebrew, 151-56; and Yahweh, 154
Euphrates River, 26, 36
Europe, 86
Evolution, 2-5, 6, 7
Exodus, 147
Ezekiel, 163

Farming, 21. *See also* Agriculture
Feudalism, 86
Fire, 14, 17

Gauls, 87
Genesis, 149-50, 156, 167-72
Germans, 87
Gideon, 122
Gilgamesh epic, 79-84, 126
God, as cause of change, 160; during the Hebrew exile, 161; as executor, 159; for all people, 165; modern, 145; and nature, 146; and Persia, 161; as prophets portrayed, 155; restoring power, 163; as revealed in history, 161; transcendent, 145. *See also* Yahweh
Gods, Assyrian, 126; Babylonian, 78, 146; and Babylonian literature, 79; Canaanite, 119, 151; and civilization, 28; early, 155; Egyptian, 61, 62, 91, 92, 98-99, 146; and Hammurabi's Code, 78; Hittite, 86; Jeremiah's attitude toward, 154; Mesopotamian, 146; origin of concept, 16; Persian, 137; power of, 79; and society's structure, 160; Sumerian, 42, 43-44, 78, 146; theme of dying, 121
Gold, 130
Golden calf story, 147
Goliath, 122, 148
Government, Assyrian, 126; Babylonian, 76-77; Egyptian, 54-57, 60, 77; Hebrew, 122-25; Hittite, 86-87; Neolithic, 23; Persian, 134-35; Sumerian, 38
Greeks, and Crete, 88-89, 90; in Near East, 131; origin of language, 86; and Persia, 139-40

Hammurabi, 77-79, 119
Hammurabi's Code, 77-78, 103-06
Hebrews, and Baal, 151; beliefs, 145; and Bible, 144; in Canaan, 119, 122, 147; collapse of government, 123; concept of divine force, 144; contribution, 146; covenant, 147-51, 162-65; in Egypt, 122; and enemies, 150; escape from Egypt, 101-102; and ethics and morality, 155; and ethics and religion, 155; in exile, 161; faith, 149-51; governed

by others, 163; government, 122-25; influence, 121-26, 165-66; and monarchy, 154-55; and monotheism, 138, 146, 147, 152; under Persia, 134; political unity, 158; and rebirth, 163-65; sense of history, 159-63; separation of religion from nature, 144-46; in slavery, 123; social and political organization, 122; social problems, 158; spiritual revolution, 124, 144-46; Sumerian influence, 42. *See also* Israel, Judah

Hellespont, 140

Herodotus, advice of Croesus to Cyrus, 134; as chronicler of Cyrus, 132; about Cyrus, 132-34; importance of, 131; on King's Highway, 135

Hierarchy, 49

Hieroglyphics, 56

Historian, 11

Hittite, assimilation, 87-88; confrontation with Egypt, 101; and Egyptian gods, 98; government, 86-87; and Hebrew strength, 123; and invasion of Egypt, 91; language, 86; nature of, 86-88; and Syria-Palestine, 119

Hominids, 3

Homo sapiens, 3-5. *See also* Humans

Horses, 86

Horus, 63, 91

Humans, adaptability of, 6-7; control of environment, 8-9; evolution, 6, 7; mind, 10-13; Paleolithic, 17-18; as primates, 3; similarities to animals, 7; spiritual problems, 11. *See also Homo sapiens*

Hyksos, 95-96

"Hymn to Aton," 99-101

Ice Age, 3

Imperial Period, 95

Inanna, 43, 155

Indo-Europeans, and feudalism, 86-87; in Iran, 131; language, 86; in Syria-Palestine, 119; tribes, 86

"Instruction for King Merikere, The," 95

"Instruction of Amen-Hotep, The," 93-94

"Instruction of the Vizer Ptah-Hotep, The," 93

Iran, 131, 137

Iron, and Assyria, 127; and civilization, 131; discovery of, 22, 114-15; importance of, 124

Iron Age, 115, 124

Iron Age Revolution, 114

Irrigation, 37, 53

Isaac, 149-50

Isaiah, 160, 165-66; quoted, 160, 161, 166, 177-78

Ishtar, as Babylonian god, 78; in Gilgamesh epic, 80; nature of, 119, 144

Isis, 62-63, 92, 120

Israel, and Assyrians, 127; and Christianity, 165; and covenant, 147-51, 162-65; and cultural revolution, 121-26; decline of, 158; enslavement of, 158-59; and exile, 161; as kingdom, 163; origin of, 123; in power, 154; prophets' view of defeat, 159; role of, 165; and salvation, 165. *See also* Hebrews

Java man, 3

Jeremiah, and Israel's punishment, 159; and new covenant, 162-63, 165; as prophet, 153-54; quoted, 153, 159, 162

Jericho, 150

Jerusalem, capture by Babylonia, 123; completion of temple, 158; Hebrew conquest of, 122; Hebrews' return to, 161

Jesus, 27, 165

Joshua, 122; Book of, 150

Judah, and Assyrians, 158; destruction, 158; origin of, 123, 158

Judges, Book of, 150

Ka, 59

Kadesh, 101

Karnak, 96

Kings, Babylonian, 76, 77; Egyptian, 101; Hittite, 86; Sumerian, 49; and war, 128

Kings, Book of, 145-46, 151-52

King's Highway, 135

Knossos, 89

Lamentation, 41

Language, and civilization, 27; Crete, 88; Hittite, 86; importance of, 6; Indo-European, 86; Phoenician, 116; Sumerian, 39-40, 76

Latin, 86

Laws, 23, 78

Lebanon, 130

Libya, 60

Linguistics, 9

Literature, Assyrian, 126; Babylonian, 79; Cretan, 89; development of, 27; Egyptian, 67; Sumerian, 40-42

Lower Egypt, 54

Lydia, civilization, 129-31; nature of, 126; and Persia, 133, 134

Magic, and Hebrew prophets, 151; and Hebrews, 145, 149; in Paleolithic era, 14-15

Man, *chart,* 29

Marathon, 139-40

Marduk, actions of, 159; as Babylonian god, 78; compared with Aton, 98; and Cyrus, 146; in myth, 79, 160; rise of, 79

INDEX 193

Medium of exchange, 130
Megiddo, 96
Memphis, 56
Menes, 54
Merchants, Babylonian, 77; and coins, 131; development of, 38; Sumerian, 49, 76
Mesolithic era, 18
Mesopotamia, Assyria in, 126; under Babylonian empire, 77; and Canaan, 119; civilization in, 76, 85, 90, 102; definition, 36; in first millennium B.C., 126; gods, 146; and Hebrew strength, 123; and origin of flood story, 84; religion in, 38; social structure, 77
Messiah, 165
Metallurgy, 22
Middle Kingdom, 91
Middle Stone Age, 18
Minos, 88
Minotaur, 89
Monotheism, conditions for, 98; and the covenant, 146-51; definition, 62, 152; in Egypt, 98; emergence of, 124, 153; Hebrew, 138; Persian, 138-39; and prophets, 151-56
Morality, definition, 11; Egyptian, 65; Hebrew, 155; and Yahweh, 154
Moses, 145, 147
Mot, 120
Mummification, 59, 93
Mythological Thought, 32-33
Mythology, Babylonian, 79; and Cretan civilization, 89; decline of, 139; Egyptian, 62-63; origin of, 24; Persian, 137; relation to civilization, 146; Semitic, 76; Sumerian, 38, 42, 42-44

Nathan, 155
Neanderthal man, 3
Near East, and Christianity, 165; in first millennium B.C., 126, 129; and Greek culture, 140; *map*, 66, 118
Negative Confession, 64-65, 155
Nehemiah, 154-55
Neolithic era, culture, 19-26; definition, 13; social change, 23; technology, 22-23
Neolithic Revolution, 19-21, 22-23, 114
New Stone Age, 13. *See also* Neolithic era
Nile River, and civilization, 52; effect on Egypt, 52-53, 159; and Egyptian view of universe, 92; isolation of valley, 53-54; original people of, 26; and pyramids, 57
Nineveh, 126, 127, 129
Nubia, 60

Old Kingdom, 56, 91
Old Stone Age, 13. *See also* Paleolithic era

Osiris, and Atonist movement, 98; and death, 93; in myth, 62-63, 92, 120; and pharaoh, 91

Paleolithic era, art, 17; culture, 13-18; definition, 13; magic in, 14-15; man during, 17-18; population, 18; religion, 14, 15-17; social structure, 14; technology, 13-14
Palestine, 134, 144, 150. *See also* Syria-Palestine
Pantheon, 42
Papyrus, 56
Passover, 160
Pastoral people, 24, 122
Patriarchs, 122
Peking man, 3
Persia, civilization of, 131-140; conquest of, 140; and Hebrew prophets, 161; later rulers, 139-40; *map*, 136; nature of, 126; political structure, 134; reasons for success, 135-36; religion, 137-39, 146
Persian Gulf, 36
Pharaoh, after Old Kingdom, 95; and dating, 92; decline of, 91; effect of Hyksos invasion on, 95; and Egyptian religion, 137; Eighteenth Dynasty, 96; form, 92; as human, 98; Menes, 54; nature of, 59, 60; nature of rule, 54; palaces, 57; power, 59; and pyramids, 59; relation to gods, 91, 93; relation to Re, 61; role, 55-56; as warriors, 101
Philistines, 122
Phoenicia, 115-19
Politics, Babylonian, 85; definition, 10; Paleolithic, 14; in studying culture, 11; Sumerian, 37-38
Polytheism, and Amenhotep, 98; Egyptian, 61, 91; reasons for, 146
Pottery, 22
Priests, and Atonist movement, 97, 98; Egyptian, 96; Paleolithic, 16; and pictographic writing, 117; Sumerian, 38, 49
Primates, 3, 5; *chart*, 4
Property, 23, 53
Prophets, 151-56, 161
Proverbs, Sumerian, 48-49; Egyptian, 67, 93; Hebrew, 176-77
Psalms, 124, 173-76
Pyramids, *chart*, 58; construction of, 57-58; and Egyptian view of universe, 92; nature of, 57-61; robbery of, 95; significance of, 59-61; as tombs, 59

Ramses II, 101
Re, 55, 59, 61, 91
Rebirth, 163-65
Religion, Assyrian, 126; Canaanite, 119;

194   INDEX

and civilization, 28; Egyptian, 61-67, 92, 97-99, 137, 146; as element of culture, 11; and ethics, 154, 155-56; Hebrew, 147, 161; nature, 23-25; Neolithic, 23-25; Paleolithic, 14, 15-17; and Paleolithic art, 17; Persian, 137-39; in Persian empire, 134; Phoenician, 116; under Semites, 76; separation from nature, 144-46; Sumerian, 38, 42-47; Zoroastrianism, 137-38
Resurrection, 63
Rhodesian man, 3
"Righteous Sufferer" Prayer, 44-47

Samuel, 154-55; quoted, 124, 148, 154, 160
Sanskrit, 86
Sarah, 149
Sardis, 133
Sargon II, 127
Satrap, 134
Saul, 122
Scribes, Egyptian, 56; origin of class, 27; and pictographic writing, 117; in Sumer, 39
Semites, 76
Shaman, 14-15
Shamash, 78
Sidon, 116
Siege tower, 127
Sin, 78
Social structure, definition, 10; Neolithic, 23; Paleolithic, 14; Sumerian, 37-38. *See also* Society
Society, Babylonian, 76, 78; and civilization, 135; definition, 10; Egyptian, 55, 56, 57, 77, 94; Hebrew, 158; Mesopotamian, 77; need for laws, 78; and religion, 16; structure of, 181-82; Sumerian, 38, 48-51; traits of, 154; urban, 27-28. *See also* Social structure
Solomon, 123, 151, 158
Spain, 116
Specialization, 38, 56
Stele, 54
"Story of Sinuhe, The," 67, 69-73
Sumer, agriculture in, 43; civilization, 67; contact with others, 76; cosmology, 42-44; culture, 38-42; education in, 39-40; geographical features, 37; gods, 146; government, 38, 49; influence on Babylonia, 86; and invasion by Semites, 76; literature, 40-42; mythology, 42-44; origin of, 36; political structure, 37-38; proverbs of, 48-49; religion, 42-47; social problems, 47-49; social structure, 37-38, 48-51; and specialization, 38; time of, 52; trade in, 38; writing, 117;

writings, 47-49; written language, 39-40
Syria, 96
Syria-Palestine, and Assyria, 127; and Canaan, 119; and Hebrew government, 122; nature of, 116

Technology, Cretan, 89-90; definition, 8; Hittite, 86; Neolithic, 22-23; Paleolithic, 13-14; in studying culture, 11; Sumerian, 48; and war, 128
Ten Commandments, 147
Thebes, 91, 95, 96
Theocracy, 38, 57, 58
Theseus, 89
Tiamat, 79, 144
Tigris River, 26, 36, 37
Tools, bronze, 115; and early man, 13; and human adaptability, 6; iron, 114; significance of, 14; use in archaeology, 17
Totem, 16
Totemism, 16, 62
Trade, 38, 56, 130
Tutmosis, 96-97, 119, 127
Tyre, 96, 116

Upper Egypt, 54, 91
Ur, 49
Urbanization, 27-28
Utnapishtim, 81, 82

Valley of the Kings, 96
Village, 23

War, and Assyria, 126-29; in Bronze Age, 115; and civilization, 77; idealistic, 129; theory of, 128-29
War chariots, 86
Weapons, 115, 127
Weather, 23
Woolley, Sir C. Leonard, 49
Writing, alphabetic, 117-19; Assyrian, 126; cuneiform, 39; development in Egypt, 56-57; early, 117, 118

Xerxes, 140

Yahweh, and Abraham, 149-50; and the covenant, 147-51; as Hebrew god, 145; and Israel's defeat, 159; nature of, 147; and prophets, 151, 152, 154. *See also* God

Ziggurats, 37
Zoroaster, 137, 146
Zoroastrianism, 137, 146